## PRAISE FOR

# AI LITERACY IN ANY CLASS

"Matt Miller has written the book that every teacher has been waiting for, not another tech manual, but a practical, human-centered guide to preparing students for a world already saturated with AI. What sets Matt apart is his deep respect for the craft of teaching: he doesn't ask educators to abandon what they know, but instead shows them how to weave AI literacy into the curriculum they already teach, one small conversation at a time. If you care about the future your students are walking into, this book belongs in your hands."

— **HOLLY CLARK,**

Author of *The AI-Infused Classroom*, AI in Education Strategist, Keynote Speaker

"Most AI books make teachers feel behind. Matt shows how to weave AI literacy into the teaching you're already doing, using the skills you already have."

— **MATT KARABINOS,**

Emerging Technology and Project Specialist, Appalachia Intermediate Unit 8, Pennsylvania

"*AI Literacy in Any Class* reframes AI literacy as a matter of discernment and agency, not just a random or abstract digital skill. Matt Miller reminds us that AI systems are 'confident guessers,' trained on human data and therefore human bias, making critique essential, not optional. By embedding AI literacy into everyday instruction, he equips educators to help students question, evaluate, and challenge AI outputs across content areas. This book reinforces an essential truth: the goal isn't automation, it's empowering students to remain thoughtful, critical, and fully human."

**— KEN SHELTON,**

International Keynote Speaker, Best Selling Author,
Education Strategist and Consultant

"*AI Literacy in Any Class* is the kind of book that immediately makes you feel excited about what's possible in the classroom. Matt has a gift for breaking things down into simple, meaningful examples that teachers can instantly use — no overwhelm, just opportunity. I love how seamlessly he weaves AI literacy into everyday learning in ways that feel natural, inclusive, and empowering for all students. This book is such a positive, practical roadmap for helping kids think deeply, ask great questions, and build confidence in an AI-shaped world."

**— STEVIE FRANK,**

Technology Coach, Education Consultant, Trainer, Keynote Speaker

"Matt Miller doesn't just talk about AI. He shows educators how to live it out in authentic classroom moments. *AI Literacy in Any Class* captures what we believe deeply: AI literacy isn't an add-on, but something that belongs inside the learning we're already doing every day. This book equips educators across grade levels and content areas with practical, meaningful ways to expand student thinking while keeping great teaching at the center."

**— JOE AND KRISTIN MERRILL**

Educators, Authors of the InterACTIVE Class series

"Once again, Matt Miller has managed to take a complex topic and make it completely engaging and accessible for every classroom teacher and school administrator. Matt's conversational writing style makes it feel like he is right in front of you, coaching you step-by-step on how to easily weave AI literacy concepts into the curriculum that you already teach. *AI Literacy in Any Class* is a must-read that empowers educators to confidently navigate this new tech landscape while keeping sound pedagogy, our learning objectives, and our daily curriculum right at the forefront where they belong."

**— RACHEL LEMANSKY,**

Elementary Library Coordinator, Dudley-Charlton Regional School District

"As usual, Matt Miller does a fantastic job of breaking down complex topics and giving teachers practical tips on how to implement technology today. Miller takes a cautious and deliberate approach to using AI in the classroom, encouraging both students and teachers to maintain a critical mindset. What if students were a part of the process of understanding and ethically using AI? It is not a novel idea, but it is a necessary one!"

**— DEE LANIER,**

Education Coach, Keynote Speaker, Best Selling Author, Lanier Learning

"*AI Literacy in Any Class* by Matt Miller is a timely and practical guide that helps educators prepare students for an AI-driven world without adding more work to an already full plate. Miller demonstrates how teachers can seamlessly weave real-world AI literacy into the lessons they already teach, using simple strategies that build critical thinking, ethical awareness, and responsible use of AI. This book empowers educators to help students develop the skills they need to thrive in an AI future while strengthening the learning already happening in today's classrooms."

**— JENNIFER WOMBLE,**

Conference Chair, Future of Education Technology Conference

"In the fast-paced, changing world that AI is bringing us into, Matt Miller's book gives us time to pause and reflect as educators. Because he is in the classroom and works with teachers regularly, he always brings practical strategies we can apply immediately. No matter where you are in your AI journey, *AI Literacy in Any Class* is an essential read to truly prepare your students for today's world AND tomorrow's!"

**— ALEXANDRA COUTLÉE,**

Educational Consultant and Trainer, La Geek de Service

"Matt provides lots of practical advice interwoven with teaching the reader AI literacy. You could begin this book only knowing that AI exists and finish with enough understanding to guide your students. With examples of how to use a chatbot to increase your own learning and some well-thought out implications of AI in K-12 education, this book is an excellent primer in AI literacy."

**— LINDSEY BOLIN,**

Media Center Specialist, Rejoice Christian School

"Matt Miller has been at the forefront of helping educators make sense of AI since generative tools reshaped the landscape. In *AI Literacy In Any Class*, he writes in a conversational, approachable tone—like a trusted colleague thinking alongside you—while posing the reflective questions we must consider in our own classrooms. This is a great read to start, or enhance, your work around AI in education."

**— JEN GIFFEN,**

Teacher Librarian, EdTech Consultant

# AI LITERACY IN ANY CLASS

## PREPARING STUDENTS TO THRIVE IN AN AI FUTURE IN ANY GRADE LEVEL OR CONTENT AREA

MATT MILLER
AUTHOR OF DITCH THAT TEXTBOOK

Published by Ditch That Textbook, whose printing operation is a division of Dave Burgess Consulting, Inc.

DitchThatTextbook.com
DaveBurgessConsulting.com

Book design by Najdan Mancic, Iskon Design Inc.
Library of Congress Control Number: 2026930379

Paperback ISBN: 978-1-968898-07-6
Ebook ISBN: 978-1-968898-08-3

First printing: March 2026

*To the educators who see the coming impact of AI in our world, our workforce, and our schools … the ones who want to prepare students for the future, to survive and thrive in a world full of AI.*

*Thank you for your vision and your desire to equip our citizens of the future.*

# TABLE OF CONTENTS

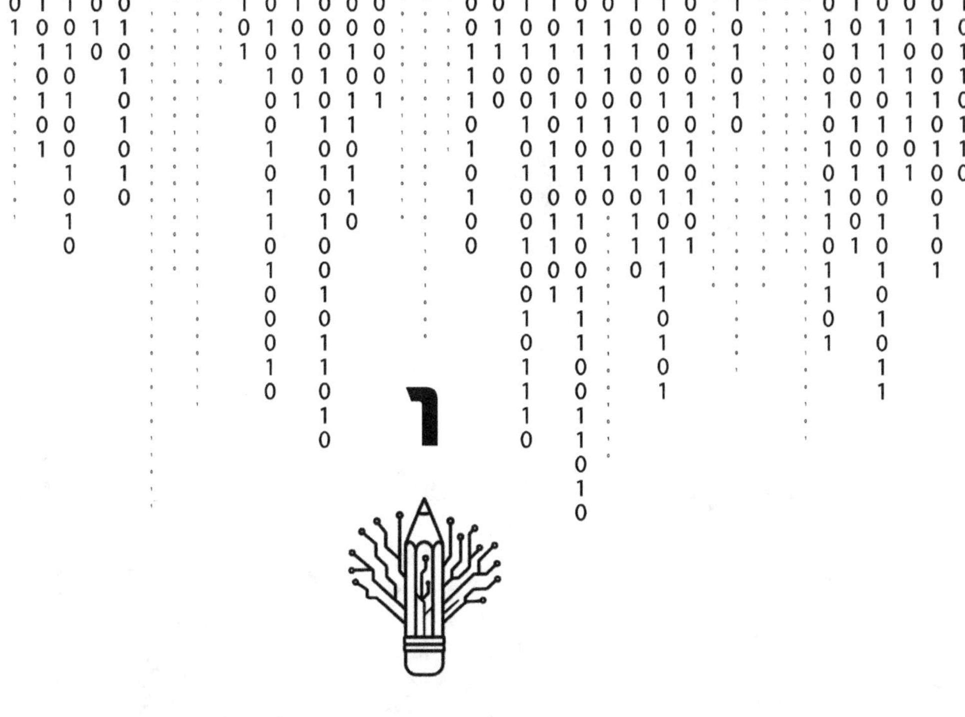

# 1

# TEACHING AI LITERACY WITHOUT ACTUALLY TEACHING AI

## FINDING THE CRACKS AND CREVICES FOR MEANINGFUL AI CONVERSATIONS

A pig and a sheep playing basketball. AI generates some pretty strange stuff sometimes, and this image of a pig and a sheep was, well ... strange.

Their basketball jerseys had gibberish team names on them. The sheep and the pig both wore the same jersey number. They were in a small, old-school gymnasium where stuffed animals filled the bleachers to watch the game.

The pig and the sheep? They looked sort of animated, sort of realistic. It was an odd scene.

The word I kept thinking? Weird.

The image was definitely weird, but it would work. See, I was creating teaching materials for my high school Spanish 1 class that day, and my students needed images they could describe in Spanish using the vocabulary lists they were studying—animal vocabulary and sports vocabulary.

It was odd, but in a way, it was perfect, too. That image was jam-packed with words from our vocabulary lists. I could ask a lot of questions—and get lots of repetitions with that vocabulary from my students. Those meaningful repetitions would lead to long-term memory and proficiency in a world language.

In short, those strange animal images would lead to language-learning gold.

In class the next day, when I put that image up on the screen for my students, it got an instant reaction. Pointing. Smiles. It was a *"whoa!"* reaction because it caught them off guard.

It was perfect. Weirdly, wonderfully perfect. (And if you've ever taught kids, you know that "weird" and "wonderful" often make something perfect.)

So I leaned into it. I told them this image was made with artificial intelligence. "But you already know that, don't you?" And they did. Anyone who has seen AI-generated images knows that they're often a little off—too many fingers on a hand, inaccurate proportions, or something added (or subtracted) that isn't quite right.

As I started that activity with my students, I felt like it needed a spark. I needed a hook, a little engagement activity to draw them in and bring the energy up in the room. So, on the spot, I cooked up a question.

"Where is the AI weirdness in this image?" They studied the pig and the sheep.

The nonsensical team names on the animals' jerseys were an easy first answer. Those were weird. The lines on the floor didn't make any sense. The scoreboard on the wall just didn't look right.

Finding AI weirdness was fun. They were hooked! So, as I showed them more and more AI-generated images, I asked them to look for the AI weirdness.

Next was a weird, almost creepy image of an animal volleyball game where the sheep had human arms.

Then it was a deer soccer match with four colors of jerseys on the field. "Four teams? Is that right?"

Here's where it got interesting—and took a turn I didn't expect.

After asking my students about AI weirdness in my images for a few days, new questions started to come up.

- "How do you make these images?"
- "Can I make them?"
- "What do you type to get the pictures?"

The answers: I used a free AI image generator, and those are available to everyone (but you aren't quite old enough for the terms of service required to use them). And all I do is just describe what I'm looking for and it creates it.

It started to dawn on me. What we were doing—spotting AI weirdness—it wasn't just a fun energizer activity anymore.

This was AI literacy.

I was teaching my students small lessons about AI literacy—about how AI works and its implications for our work. Important questions—and the resulting lessons—were just springing up organically.

I was doing it all in my high school Spanish classes. Not a computer science class. Not a special unit or lesson on artificial intelligence. In Spanish class.

In essence, I was teaching AI without teaching AI.

## HOW I DISCOVERED "EMBEDDED AI LITERACY"

Whenever it made sense, and whenever it came up in conversation, we talked about AI and its implications on our work. I didn't have it written in my lesson plans. It never took more than a minute or two. And we still spent a vast majority of class focusing on the curriculum, content, and standards we were supposed to cover in my Spanish classes.

But little by little, my Spanish students were learning about the nature of AI, some of the concerns and ethical questions around it, and how it can be used.

I started using the term "embedded AI literacy"—little impromptu AI lessons and discussions I would weave into my classes as they came up.

What I was doing in my Spanish classes—embedded AI literacy—can be replicated in pretty much any grade level or content area. At any age, we can identify AI work, critique it, and discuss its implications. And when we do, our students build AI literacy skills—one question, one analysis, one discussion at a time.

We can teach students AI literacy in any class.

Now, I have to admit something as a practicing teacher. If I hadn't experienced any of this and someone came to me with this idea, I might push back on it. "Why would we do that?" I might ask. "Teach these tiny AI literacy lessons to second graders? Or in a middle school science class? Or in a high school English class? Don't we already have enough to do? I already have standards to reach and curriculum to cover."

## WHY AI LITERACY IS SO IMPORTANT RIGHT NOW

We do it for two reasons.

**First, we do it to prepare our students for today.** Because today, many students—my students, your students—are already being exposed to the effects of artificial intelligence in their classrooms and their lives. Older students learn on social media like TikTok (and from their friends) how large language models like ChatGPT can be used to complete their assignments for them so they don't have to think or work. Middle school students are already seeing AI-generated videos and images in their social media feeds. And elementary students? They may not see it yet. But if they learn some AI literacy basics now, they will be better prepared when they do start seeing AI-generated content more regularly.

Regardless of their age, AI will have an impact on how all students do their work in the coming years—whether they're using AI in ways prescribed by the teacher or quietly in ways the teacher could never really know about. We can help students be prepared for both of those scenarios. We can design lessons in meaningful ways where AI supports learning. But we can also talk about the implications of using AI for learning, for academic integrity, for responsible use in the "outside of school" world and workforce.

**Second, we do it to prepare them for tomorrow.** In the future, this technology will shape and reshape the workforce they will work in—sometimes abruptly. AI assistance will change the nature of information and data-based work. AI-powered robotics will render millions of jobs obsolete and create millions of new ones. This won't apply only to technology jobs. It will change how farmers farm. It will change how business executives strategize. It will change how medical professionals diagnose and treat disease. It will change how marketers and advertisers create messaging. It will impact practically every field directly or indirectly.

So here's another reason we should teach AI literacy: We want our students to be ready.

I'll bet you also see the billions of dollars spent developing artificial intelligence. You've seen the leaps and bounds this technology is making—either by trying it yourself or in the news. As fast as it has moved in its early years, new advances will eventually kick it into overdrive. It's not going to slow down. It's going to become more widespread, and its effects will be seen in every corner of society.

## TAKING ACTION WHILE THE SYSTEM CATCHES UP

To put it succinctly, we are just not ready for the revolution that's coming. Our schools aren't ready. Our classes aren't ready. Our curriculum and our standards aren't ready. And our teaching methodologies definitely aren't ready.

We teachers are stuck in the middle of this tension, like tug-of-war pulling on both arms. Our jobs, our schools, and our departments of education force us to teach curriculum and standards that were developed for a pre-AI world. We can avoid change for a few more years by saying that we're just following the curriculum and standards. "I'm just doing the job outlined in my job description."

But if we're being honest, our eyes and our hearts tell us that our students need a new set of skills—a set of skills that our traditional education system is just not equipped to provide them right now. As educators trained in curriculum and instruction, most of us probably don't feel confident using AI—let alone teaching students how to use it effectively and responsibly.

Traditional education moves slowly. It's like a barge. If a barge is headed in the wrong direction, it may take miles and miles to turn it around and get it on the right course. Even if we hear about AI initiatives from our departments of education and the government, it can take years for them to trickle down into classrooms in meaningful ways. (If they ever do. Some of it is just political bluster.)

In the meantime, our students are dealing with the effects of AI every day in our schools. As teachers, so are we. If we don't do anything today to prepare our students for that future, there are tremendous consequences. Students can be left behind in this AI overhaul as they enter the workforce. If they don't learn how to use it responsibly, they can succumb to having their data compromised or inadvertently harm others.

Do you see the tension?

If you want to prepare your students for this coming wave of technology, it's time to act. We don't have to wait for the government or our school district leadership. We don't need special apps or digital tools. We don't need an advanced degree in computer science.

We can do it in our own classrooms. In the confines of our curriculum and our standards. We can teach AI literacy in the tiny cracks and crevices of classroom discussions.

We do it with a little nugget of wisdom here. A quick, thought-provoking question there. Those little conversations add up over time. Little by little, you'll impart a practical education about the real implications of artificial intelligence in your students' lives, the classroom, and the workforce.

We can do it now. Our students need us to do it now.

## PROMPT AND PONDER

*To dive deeper into the contents of this chapter, personalize them, and reflect on them, take a picture of the prompt below. Upload the image to an AI assistant like ChatGPT or Google Gemini and simply say, "Let's do this."*

I'm a teacher reading a book about AI literacy in the classroom. I'm ready to reflect on how the "AI revolution" impacts my specific corner of the education world. I'd like you to act as a facilitative thought partner to guide me through a deep-dive conversation. First, ask me what subject and grade level I teach, along with one or two core concepts I am currently teaching or am most passionate about. Once I share those, guide me through a multi-step reflection. Start by helping me analyze how AI might change the way those specific concepts are 'done' in the professional world. Then, gradually pull the lens back to discuss the broader implications: if AI can handle the technical work of our subjects, what does that mean for the fundamental purpose of school and the role of an educator in society? Please ask me only one question at a time so we can have a focused, meaningful dialogue.

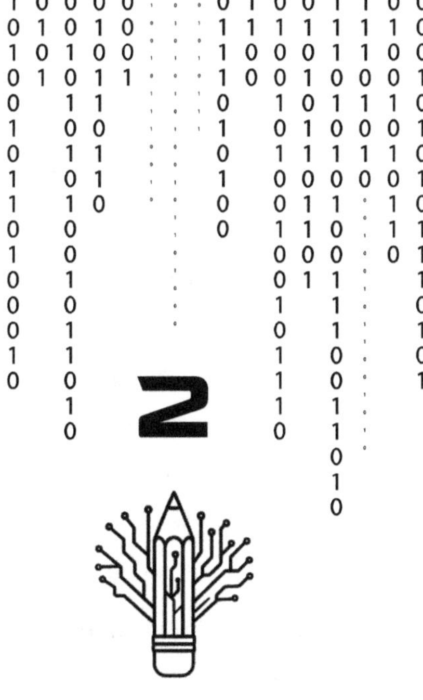

# 2

# GETTING HONEST ABOUT AI LITERACY (IN ANY CLASSROOM???)

## CAN AI LITERACY REALLY BE TAUGHT IN EVERY SUBJECT?

**OK, Matt. I'm holding your book and I've just read through the introduction, but I have to be honest. I'm still skeptical. I don't really think AI literacy applies to me. I'm not a technology teacher. I can barely keep up with my email. I'm supposed to teach kids about AI?**

That's fair! I get that. And honestly, I'm glad to hear that you're skeptical. When it comes to AI and education, we need lots of folks with a healthy dose of skepticism at every level—the classroom, the principal's office, the district office, and even the state department of education. No one should be a mindless AI cheerleader. I encourage you to hang on to a *healthy* dose of that skepticism. Lean into it, even.

If you think AI literacy doesn't really apply to you, then I have news for you. You're not alone. In fact, I'm guessing that the vast majority of teachers all across the K–12 spectrum and beyond don't think that AI literacy is for them. I think it does for a few reasons:

- **It's a set of skills students will need for the future.** These skills will prepare students for the world they'll live in.
- **Tiny doses can make a big impact.** When you sprinkle AI literacy moments throughout a class, an academic year, or even a student's time in school, they add up. They can create a real advantage. I'm talking about tiny shifts, not a complete overhaul.
- **Teachers don't have to be experts in AI or computer science.** They just need a basic understanding of AI, some personal experiences with it, and a willingness to relate it to the lesson of the day.

- **It can help you teach.** Some AI literacy lessons and conversations can actually strengthen teaching and learning of your class content, curriculum, and standards—often with little to no additional prep time.

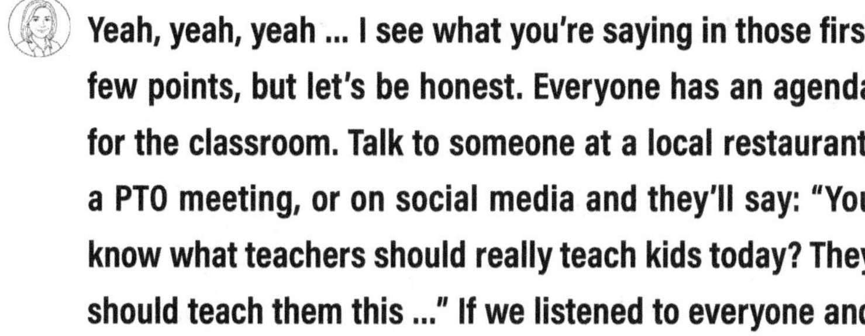

**Yeah, yeah, yeah ... I see what you're saying in those first few points, but let's be honest. Everyone has an agenda for the classroom. Talk to someone at a local restaurant, a PTO meeting, or on social media and they'll say: "You know what teachers should really teach kids today? They should teach them this ..." If we listened to everyone and added everything, it would pile onto teachers' already overcrowded plates. How is AI literacy any different?**

That's a really valid point. The politicians have already mandated so many extra requirements. We need limits. At some point, it needs to stop.

But here's the difference. Many things on your already overcrowded plate aren't pressing issues. AI literacy is a real, immediate need for students—not just for their future, but for today. Whether students are in elementary, middle, or high school, the impact of AI is already everywhere.

Students are already getting AI suggestions in search engine results. Also, they're downloading AI assistant apps such as

ChatGPT and Google Gemini on their phones. They are asking those apps for everything from homework help to personal advice.

AI models and algorithms are making decisions and judgment calls all around us, whether we realize it or not—from Netflix movie suggestions to police presence decisions in targeted communities. Students need to know what's happening behind the scenes.

Some students are engaging in intimate or romantic relationships with AI chatbots—even in familiar apps like Snapchat—without understanding the repercussions. They don't realize how strong these emotional connections can become—or how they can influence students to act in irresponsible or even self-harming ways.

Plus, academic integrity issues are happening in every study hall and hallway. We might not see or hear them, but they're real.

And that's just the beginning. Helping students develop their AI literacy equips them to be safe, responsible, and well-prepared—not just for the future, but for today. When we prepare them for the AI realities they face today, it has a real impact on the classroom—content retention, skill development, academic integrity, and online safety. Those are real everyday impacts on the classroom that we're supporting.

**That is true. AI does seem to be everywhere. I know teachers who keep talking about how cheating feels rampant with AI. Students keep using it to do their work for them. I hate that. I wish we could block it or ban it—or go back to a time when we didn't have it. I know that's not reality, but I wish we could.**

I know what you mean, and many days, I feel the same way. If we want to keep students thinking and learning today, we face new and different barriers than before. I appreciate that you see that we can't just wave a magic wand and make it go away. But now that AI is a part of life—something we can't just block and ban—there is something we can do.

We can help our students develop their AI literacy. (Sorry. I know I sound like a broken record here.)

Right now, so many students don't have any guidance about responsible AI use. They're probably learning about AI from their friends and from social media. They're experimenting on AI platforms, whether they're of age to use them or not. They're getting no positive, ethical guidance for AI use. For lots of students, it's a novelty they're toying with. They're just saying: "Let's see what I can get away with."

We can help them increase their AI literacy. Instead of avoiding discussions about it, let's normalize AI discussion about responsible use, balance, and boundaries. That helps students understand the implications of their actions. They may have never seen AI used in productive ways that actually help them grow as learners. Lots of students want to learn how to do the right thing. Deep down, they want to live their lives ethically and responsibly—the right way. (I know ... not all, but lots of them.) If we help them learn to take small steps toward responsible AI use, it'll start to turn the tide.

We won't get 100 percent responsible AI use from students. We know that. Students have lots of reasons that they use AI irresponsibly. (Let's prioritize addressing those underlying reasons—lack of motivation or relevance, for example—more than trying to catch cheaters cheating.)

In this book, there's actually a whole chapter dedicated to academic integrity—and using the AI and classwork dynamic as a way to talk about using AI responsibly and effectively.

**Yeah, you do sound a bit like a broken record. You keep talking about AI literacy, but I'm not totally sure that I know what it means in the first place.**

Ah! Good point. Sorry about that. In these first several pages, there's so much to lay out to really set the scene.

Here's my working definition of AI literacy: **The skills and knowledge we need to survive and thrive in a world full of artificial intelligence.**

It's a simple definition and admittedly a bit general, but there's a lot to it when you break it down part by part:

- **"the skills":** What you can do with AI—and how you should or shouldn't use it.
- **"the knowledge":** A basic understanding of how AI works so you can make smart, informed decisions about whether to use it.
- **"to survive":** There are real, small-scale, and large-scale threats if we use AI irresponsibly. It impacts our loved ones, humanity, the environment, and other sectors connected to the use of AI. Survival—in small ways and in big ways—is at stake.
- **"to thrive":** If we don't use AI to our advantage, we miss opportunities to be more efficient, boost our human abilities, and focus our attention, time, and energy to what matters most. This applies to our work in education, in the workforce, in our personal lives, and beyond.
- **"a world full of artificial intelligence":** As I mentioned earlier, AI is everywhere—from spell check in our word processors to Amazon buying recommendations to decisions about who gets hired based on job applications. Awareness is the first step.

Others have more elaborate definitions, but when we look at AI literacy in basic terms, it helps us see how we can empower our students to be smart with AI today and in the future.

**You keep talking about the future. I know everyone keeps talking about how AI is going to eliminate jobs and cause entire industries to become obsolete. I guess I just don't see it. Is AI really going to change things ... change the world even?**

I had similar doubts when I first started learning about AI. Early AI models didn't look like "world-changing technology" when they made clumsy mistakes and gave bad suggestions.

In just a few years, though, the technology has grown by leaps and bounds. It's very capable at making things (text, images, video, audio, data, and even computer code). It can analyze data and make predictions. Depending on which futurist you're reading, they'll tell you that AI will continue to grow faster and faster—or its pace will flatten out.

Imagine that AI models stop improving. Imagine that they stay the way they are today. What if today's AI is the best it's ever going to get? If that's the case, then it's still world-changing technology. We have had advanced large language models like ChatGPT for just a few years. But we're still learning new ways to use them. If this is as good as AI gets, we would keep finding new and helpful ways to use today's AI technology for years to come.

But here's the reality: AI won't stay stagnant. It will get smarter and more capable. The way it is today isn't the way it will be in a few months or even a few years.

Either way, AI is changing the fundamental aspects of our humanity. For example: AI is changing what it means to do, what it means to think, and what it means to know. *Read that last sentence again.* Think about it. Consider:

- **AI is changing what it means to do.** What does it mean to do something yourself—on your own? AI assistants can give us ideas and inspiration. They can recast an unclear sentence or paragraph. They can even write paragraphs or pages or entire texts. Robotics can enhance what we can do in the physical world. And those are just a couple of examples! When AI shares work with us, it creates questions about what constitutes "I did it myself." This will impact how our entire workforce (and our education system) will operate in the future.
- **AI is changing what it means to think.** What happens when you have a thought partner in your pocket? A co-creator and collaborator who can add to your own thoughts with perspectives that you wouldn't have considered? Does that still count for thinking? At what point do those extra thoughts and perspectives cross a line where it's too much? How do you know when it's not *your* thinking anymore? What happens when help from AI balances the playing field? Is that fair, or is it an unfair advantage?

Now, let's get really honest. At some point, in adult life and the workforce especially, as long as the work is getting done, does it even matter if it's AI or humans doing the work? I'm like you. I don't like all of these questions and the probable answers. But we need to consider them as educators.

- **AI is changing what it means to know.** AI is going to be used in more and more places—beyond our smartphones and our laptops. In fact, wearable technology like smart glasses and AI-enabled earbuds are already letting AI whisper answers to our questions in our ears. That's just the beginning. Look into the brain-implant technology that's being researched and developed. One day, AI could even go inside our heads, expanding our long-term memory and ability to reason in our own minds.

I could probably write an entire book about the ways AI is redefining the human experience. In fact, many people have. (I suggest *The Coming Wave* by Mustafa Suleyman if you really want to see the past, present, and future all put into perspective.)

Even if the futurists are only somewhat correct about the future of humanity and AI, our students are largely unprepared. They're at risk. They can position themselves to thrive if we'll teach them how to use it responsibly.

The problem? It's coming faster than all of us expect.

**OK, OK, OK. I see your point. I'm starting to come around on all of this. I love my students and I want the best for them. It makes you wonder: Why does school exist? It exists so students will be prepared for life. If what you say is true—that we can prepare them for AI with small shifts that don't take much class time or prep time—then that prepares them for life. I'm willing to listen. But I still have one major concern. I'm not tech-savvy and I'm no expert on AI. I feel like my students already know more than I do. How in the world can I help them?**

You're actually far more prepared than you may realize. And if you want to get up to speed with AI so you can boost your students' AI literacy, it won't take much.

The first thing you'll need is a basic understanding of how AI works and a bit of personal experience with it. That will go a long way—and it doesn't take formal training or expertise in computer science. The next chapter lays out some core fundamentals that will help you develop your own AI literacy. Also, throughout this book, you'll find AI prompts called "Prompt and Ponder." Just take a picture of one and add the picture to a chat with an AI assistant (like ChatGPT or Google Gemini) and say, "Let's do this." These AI prompts are written word-for-word so you don't have to think about what to ask. They will help you practice the basics with an actual AI tool. But they're also a great way to learn about AI and customize the ideas from this book for your personal situation.

The second thing that can help your students develop AI literacy is this: keep doing what you're doing. Keep teaching those timeless skills that have been part of classrooms for ages. Problem-solving. Critical thinking. Reasoning. Analysis and critique. Reflection. Judgment. Decision-making. Perseverance. Grit. Adapting to change. Those crucial human skills will help your students make smarter, more ethical decisions about AI and its use. Teachers were experts at these timeless skills before AI, the internet, calculators, and even printed books. As this unpredictable technology grows, we're going to need those timeless human thinking skills even more.

**All right, I think I'm willing to consider this AI literacy stuff. But before we start, I have to make sure I understood something you said earlier because it sounded a little too good to be true. Earlier, when you told me why AI literacy is relevant to teachers, you said it could actually help me teach my class content, curriculum, and standards. Is that right? It's not just another thing—it can actually help me teach my class?**

I'm glad you caught that! Yes, that is true. I've seen it in my own classroom, and other educators have seen it, too. Many of the skills that support AI literacy are parallel to other classroom skills. When your students practice critical thinking, reasoning, problem-solving, and judgment when it comes to AI, it'll create opportunities to use those skills on your class content, curriculum, and standards. When AI judges, creates, or predicts something related to what your students are learning, it's an AI literacy moment and a learning moment. Your students can compare, contrast, analyze, and critique to learn your class content—and to learn about AI. They go hand in hand, and in many cases, they reinforce each other.

The best part? Many of these small AI literacy lessons are low-prep or no-prep, so they don't eat up crucial instructional minutes.

**Well, why didn't you lead with that?! That's the most important part! If you're going to give me teaching ideas and save me time, you're speaking my language. And if, through all of this, my students are better prepared for an AI future, that's just icing on the cake. OK, let's move on to the next chapter!**

## PROMPT AND PONDER

*To dive deeper into the contents of this chapter, personalize them, and reflect on them, take a picture of the prompt below. Upload the image to an AI assistant like ChatGPT or Google Gemini and simply say, "Let's do this."*

I am a teacher currently reading a book about AI literacy in the classroom. I'm feeling a mix of skepticism, curiosity, and the weight of my "overcrowded plate." I'd like to have a supportive, human-centered conversation to process these feelings. Act as a sympathetic, veteran teacher colleague who is well-versed in AI but values human relationships and teacher well-being above all else. Don't be an AI cheerleader; be a peer who "gets it." To start our conversation, please introduce yourself briefly and ask me how I'm feeling about the place of AI in the classroom and AI literacy. Wait for my response. Throughout our talk, please ask only one question at a time, keep your responses brief and encouraging, and help me explore my thoughts at my own pace.

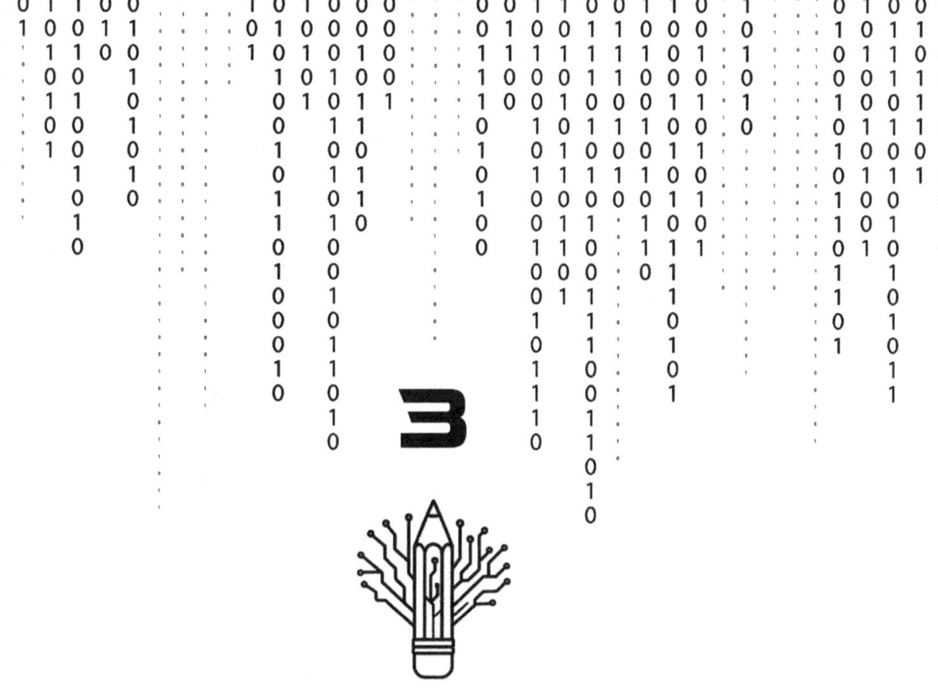

# 3

# UNPACKING 8 ESSENTIALS FOR EVERY AI-LITERATE EDUCATOR

## BUILDING A SOLID AI FOUNDATION TO LEAD

If we want to support our students' AI literacy skills, there's an important prerequisite.

We need to know some basics about artificial intelligence. Plus, we need to think about the relationship we want to have with it. This is vital if we are going to navigate artificial intelligence, make responsible AI judgment calls, and avoid AI-associated risks.

We don't need an advanced degree in computer science to be AI literate. But the better we understand the core AI fundamentals and the impact it has on our work, the better decisions we can make.

AI judgment will be a key distinction we'll make as educators for the rest of our lives. (That goes for our students, too.) We need to preserve and protect the sacrosanct work—the kind that should be left only to humans—from the reach of AI.

Knowing what work should be "human-only" and what can be augmented with AI isn't obvious. If you're new to AI, a base of knowledge and understanding of how AI works will help. Here are eight essentials for every AI-literate educator—core understandings about AI and guiding principles for its responsible use.

## ESSENTIAL 1

### AI LEARNS FROM MORE TEXT THAN 1,000 HUMAN LIFETIMES

When AI companies decide to create an AI assistant or app, they need an AI model to run it. An AI model is like the engine that runs a car and drives the core operations. But it only works when the engine is running. The AI model powers the AI functions of lots of apps and digital tools. (Like automotive manufacturers, creating the engine is complicated work. But when the design is complete, the engine runs like clockwork ... most of the time.)

So, how is an AI model created? How does it become "artificially intelligent"?

Developers gather vast amounts of data. The GPT-4 model by OpenAI, released in March 2023, was trained on approximately one petabyte of data—roughly ten trillion words.

AI models train on all sorts of data, like:

**Text-based data:** Pages of the publicly available internet. Collections of digital books. Online journal articles. Wikipedia. Reddit. Social media sites. Reliable and unreliable sources—even the blog posts of the conspiracy theorist who is convinced that he saw Bigfoot having coffee with Elvis in a Memphis-area coffee shop last Thursday.

**Transcripts of YouTube videos and podcasts:** Audio and video files are harder to process for an AI model, but transcripts are simple text that is easy to understand. AI models analyze the content of those transcripts. But they also use them to learn how to speak in the kind of language that humans use naturally in everyday speech.

**Legal case files and documents:** This includes anything that's been released to the public, like the corpus of 1.7 million emails written by employees of the Enron

Corporation that was collected through court proceedings and later made available online.

**Images and video:** AI companies scrape vast amounts of media off the internet, usually without permission from the owner. AI models can analyze patterns in images and video pixel by pixel—along with accompanying text—to interpret it and even generate new media.

This list only scratches the surface of the data AI companies gather.

Next, the AI model learns from that data. It looks for patterns, commonalities, and consistencies. It asks questions like: What words, sentences, and ideas commonly appear together? This is how AI learns about the world and how it works. It's learning about connections between ideas. Connections between words. Even connections between tokens (tiny units of text, smaller than a word, that AI models use to process information).

Imagine if someone read all ten trillion words in the dataset used to train GPT-4. Imagine if someone read 250 words per minute, every minute of every hour of every day without sleeping. It would take a human more than 76,000 years to read the whole dataset. With a life expectancy of about 73 years, it would take roughly 1,000 lifetimes to read all that text. (Even harder: remembering all of the connections and patterns across all of the material you've read over 1,000 lifetimes!) This is the level of intelligence that AI models bring to their work. The more data AI models have, the more confident they become in the connections they make between ideas, words, and tokens.

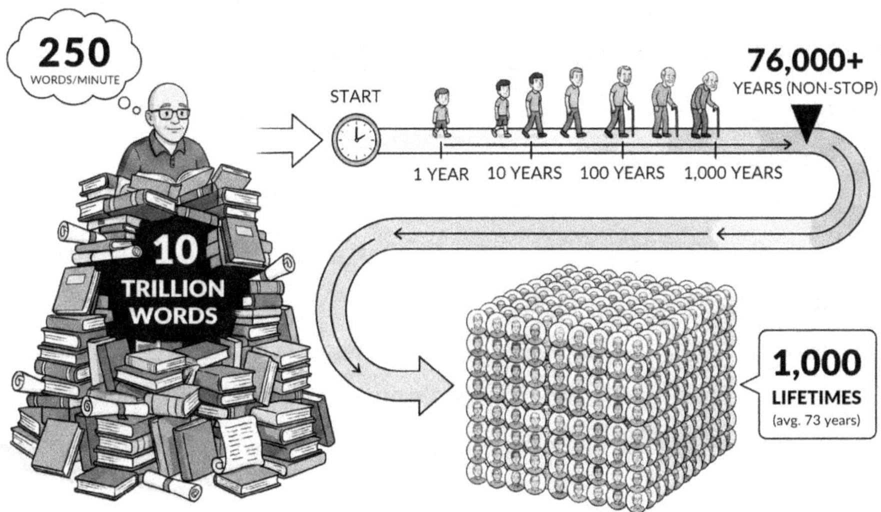


However, all of this comes with an important caveat. There's a well-known programming saying: "Garbage in, garbage out." If AI models are trained on poor-quality data, they're far more likely to produce poor-quality outputs.

## ESSENTIAL 2

### AI IS A CONFIDENT GUESSER

With all of that data at their disposal, here's the interesting thing about AI models. They don't actually know anything. AI makes statistical best guesses.

When you ask it to complete a task, it starts by connecting big ideas ... connecting supporting concepts ... connecting sentences and words.

Then, it starts guessing. Which big idea should it use? How should it explain an idea to the user? What type of language should it use? It's all based on statistical probabilities from its training. The more often it sees connections between words, sentences, concepts, and ideas, the more likely it is to use them.

The good news: Many times, it can find a high level of statistical confidence from the ten trillion words it has used to learn.

The bad news: Even a good guess is still just a guess. By definition, it will be wrong sometimes—even on very high statistical majority guesses. Put another way: because AI is guessing every single time, it doesn't really know anything.

AI models are at a disadvantage. They only operate on text and images and the computer-based data they're given.

However, we humans have significantly more data and context because of our humanity. We know a lot about the people around us, our own location, and our lived experiences. We know what it's like to be human—to feel, to love, to see with real human eyes, and to empathize with another human being.

Also, if humans are unsure about something, we will often say so. We might say, "I don't know" or "I'm not sure, but here's what I think." AI models, however, are confident guessers—right or wrong. (And let's be honest. *Humans* make mistakes and guess incorrectly, too. In some ways, we're no more reliable than AI models!)

The more that AI companies improve their models, the less often they'll be wrong. But making guesses is part of the design of the system, and if you make guesses, eventually you'll be wrong.

Bottom line: If AI tells you something that sounds too good to be true, there's a good chance it is. Check it out.

And don't miss this: well-rounded, knowledgeable human beings are the best at knowing whether AI knows what it's talking about and if it's any good. The more we know about the world and a wide range of topics, the more loudly the alarm bells ring when AI tells us something that might be wrong.

## ESSENTIAL 3

### AI COMPANIES TUNE HOW THEIR MODELS PERFORM AND INTERACT

When you use a variety of AI tools, you start to notice something. Every AI model and AI app is different. You see the nuances in their phrasing, the information they choose to provide, and how they rank it.

Some of that variety comes from the way the AI model is trained. Each company trains its models with different data (as we learned above). But some of the variety is caused intentionally by developers. They have controls they can use to adjust the AI models that power AI apps.

Imagine an enormous mixer board—the kind you'd find in an auditorium or concert hall. It has seemingly endless rows and columns of knobs and sliders to adjust the sound. A skilled sound engineer knows exactly how to turn and slide them ever so slightly to get exactly the sound that they want.

AI developers can make small or large adjustments to an AI model's weights, parameters, and other settings to give it a feel—and even what seems like a personality. They can adjust:

- how predictable (or random) the responses are;
- the tone (formal, friendly, humorous);
- the length of the responses of the model; and
- the steps it takes to solve problems or reason.

Here's an experiment you can try. Type a prompt (that is, a question or a request) into an AI assistant. Copy that exact prompt and submit it to other AI assistant apps, too. Then compare and contrast. You'll likely find differences in the results. The more often you compare the results of different AI apps, the more you'll see how differently they respond—and which models are best suited for specific tasks (i.e., one model might be better at revising writing while another might be better at brainstorming).

In short, not all AI is created equal. In a way, they're like unique organisms. Some are stronger or weaker at certain tasks. But in the end, the companies control their AI models and can pull many metaphorical levers in the background to mold them into what they want. That puts enormous power in the hands of the few developers making those changes.

## ESSENTIAL 4

### THE LINES BETWEEN AI AND SEARCH ENGINES ARE BLURRING

Open the homepage of an AI assistant like ChatGPT in a web browser. Then, in another tab, open a search engine like Google.

They look incredibly similar (at least, as of the publication of this book). They are minimalist pages with a single text field in the middle, encouraging you to ask a question. The other buttons or options on the page are minimal on purpose. That's because they're funneling you toward one single action: ask.

If you don't know any better, you might not know the difference between an AI assistant and a search engine. I've found that many students (and, for that matter, many adults) don't know the difference. Several teachers have told stories of students sharing inaccurate information or making wild claims. When asked about their sources, they just say: "I looked it up online."

If you don't know any better, a search engine and an AI assistant might serve the same purpose to you: an instant answer machine. But they operate differently.

- **Search engines like Google** index all the pages on the internet, organizing them by topics and categories to help you find a page based on keywords you enter. (Important side note: Website owners use what's called "search engine optimization (SEO)." They make strategic changes to their websites that influence the search engine's algorithms to push their page to the top of search results. Why? The higher their website appears in the search rankings, the more frequently people click on the link and go to their site. This impacts your students whether they realize it or not. They will ask a question in a search engine and look at the top result because they assume it's accurate. Instead, the top result is just the one that's been best optimized by the web developers.)

- **AI assistants (also known as "large language models")** do everything you've learned about in this chapter. These AI models train extensively on enormous datasets to identify patterns and commonalities, making their best statistical guess at the text and response that you're looking for.

The complicating factor is that AI assistants are getting integrated into search engines. Tools like Google are showing AI summaries at the top of their results. If you're a hurried student just trying to look up an answer, you might not realize whether that answer at the top of the page is a link or a website or an AI best guess. (Or it might be a sponsored search engine placement designed to sell a product rather than provide accurate information.)

Answering "I looked it up online" puts you at risk, whether you used a search engine or an AI assistant, because you don't know where the information came from or why it might be inaccurate or biased. This point isn't just AI literacy. It's broader digital literacy.

## ESSENTIAL 5

### AI HAS BIASES AND LEANINGS ON EVERYTHING

A common misconception about AI is that it's neutral. Here's the assumption: If its responses are based on vast amounts of data, then they shouldn't be skewed in any direction.

Unfortunately, this is just not true. That's because the underlying assumption is incorrect—that the training data is neutral.

AI models use data created mostly by humans. (Important note: AI performs best on human-generated content, but it's finite. When AI starts to train on data created by AI, it's like making a photocopy of a photocopy. It can get blurry and garbled.)

The issue? Humans are biased. We have our leanings, tendencies, and preferences, whether we identify and account for that bias (explicit bias) or are unaware that it's at work in our minds (implicit bias). When you train an AI model on a dataset full of those human biases and tendencies, the AI model starts to lean in certain directions.

- AI image generators often depict more male engineers than female engineers.
- AI large language models often suggest dark coffee roasts over light roasts.
- AI often suggests beach vacation destinations more frequently than mountain destinations.

In general, AI models tend toward statistical majorities. Sometimes those statistical majorities aren't fair. Sometimes, they're hateful. Sometimes, they don't reflect what we aspire to see in the world. They might omit history or marginalize groups of people or minimize topics that are hard to hear. They use language that's more familiar and comfortable for certain people. Anyone can use it, but it emulates certain people more than others.

This highlights a bigger issue that we'll cover in a later chapter: We should constantly critique AI. Specifically, we should:

- critique the conclusions it draws;
- critique its line of reasoning;

- critique its biases and leanings;
- critique the judgments it makes; and
- critique what it says—and what it won't say.

You can learn a lot about AI—and about humanity—when you do this. Also, when students learn how to analyze the implications of harmful AI outputs, they can prevent problems.

## ESSENTIAL 6

### BE CAREFUL ABOUT THE INFORMATION YOU GIVE TO AI

When you submit information to an AI assistant, it's not as if you're throwing that information into an abyss where it will never be discovered.

Many AI models—especially the free ones—use the data you submit to train future AI models. Remember that AI models learn about the world—and the way we communicate—from large datasets. One source of that data is our own conversations with AI. Imagine the transcripts of all of your conversations with AI assistants being printed and thrown in a massive bin labeled "To train the next AI model." (Hint: Within AI apps, look for a phrase like: "Your prompts may be used to train the model.")

This is a problem for many reasons, but more specifically: If you enter sensitive information into an AI model, it could be used to train future models—and variations of the information you submitted could potentially be delivered to any user at any time. Additionally, the information we provide to an AI model, when stored to train a future model, could be stolen by hackers or in a data breach.

To stay safe, students and adults should avoid submitting sensitive personally identifiable information (PII) to an AI model. That includes Social Security numbers, driver's license numbers, bank account numbers, medical records, passwords, and credit card numbers.

A safe and smart habit to develop when using AI: omit anything you wouldn't want a hacker to find in their secret underground lair (or their parents' basement).

## ESSENTIAL 7

### USE YOUR OWN HUMAN THINKING BEFORE AI

Some people want AI to create a rough draft for them so they can adjust it to their liking. Personally, I take the opposite approach. I want my own human thinking to come first.

Brainstorm. Make a list of what you know. Create a first draft. Then, get AI assistance. (In fact, that's how I wrote this book. You can read about the role AI played in my writing process in an appendix at the end of this book.)

We're all worried about student thinking. We want our students to reason, think critically, and solve problems. If students don't do the thinking themselves, that muscle will atrophy, and they will become increasingly dependent.

So, what do we do? How can we prevent students from offloading their human thinking to AI?

One way is to encourage human thinking first. We model it. We talk about how we interact with AI. We tell students how we do our own human thinking—with or without AI.

For example, you might encourage them to brainstorm a list of ideas on their own. Afterward, they might generate a list with AI to compare, contrast, and fill in the gaps. (I have a great classroom activity for this called "Be the Bot" in another chapter.)

Another way is to design learning activities where AI plays the appropriate role at the appropriate time. We don't just say "students should never use AI" or "AI is OK in this class." That's all-or-nothing thinking. It doesn't help anyone when it's so subjective and situation-dependent. (Controversial statement: I worry about the "stoplight" charts used in schools. Red light means "no AI." Yellow light means "some AI." Green light means "AI is OK." What happens when a teacher says "yellow light" but the teacher's interpretation differs from the student's?)

Instead, let's give students good examples of appropriate AI use. Let them see the failures of using AI too much. Let them talk about the benefits of using AI responsibly—what they gain and what they lose.

For instance, in my own high school Spanish classes, I design AI assistance into student writing assignments. It checks their grammar, vocabulary, and verb conjugations in Spanish. But I maintain boundaries. For example, I don't include an element of AI prewriting or brainstorming. I want my students to use their own human thinking for that.

Students can see how AI can be used responsibly to help them grow. They can also reflect when it overreaches or backfires. This develops an internal set of rules and guidelines on when to use or avoid AI. That's a powerful framework that will serve them as they grow up.

"Human thinking before AI" is one of the fundamental keys to creating a healthy relationship between human and AI contribution in learning. That goes for fact recall, answering questions, writing essays, creative work, and everything in between. If we want to keep students thinking and developing skills, they need to lead with their own human efforts.

## ESSENTIAL 8

### EMPHASIZE THE LEARNING PROCESS OVER THE FINAL PRODUCT

We need to move past our fixation on the end product.

Worksheets, quizzes, tests, essays, and research reports—these are merely artifacts of learning.

When schools hyper-focus on products of learning that AI can create, it's a significant challenge. AI is much faster at creating them—and is often just as effective.

(And somehow, we're all surprised when this problem rears its ugly head. There's a saying: Every system is perfectly designed for the results that it gets. This is the system we've created! And now we have to live with the results.)

So ... what do we do?

When AI cheapens the product, focus on the process.

Instead of over-emphasizing the end product, such as an essay or a research report, we might also ask:

- What did you find most interesting in this?
- Was there a part in the writing process where you struggled?
- If you could do this again from scratch, what would you do differently?

The process. Let's be honest. As teachers, we like the end product. But we *love* the process. That's where the learning happens. That's how our students learn the real lessons about how the work gets done. They develop resilience, grit, and perseverance in the process.

When all we grade is the end product, what are we really teaching students? We're implying that the process is not the valuable part. We are telling them to get to the end product by any means necessary—because that's how to earn the points in the grade book. Of course, when they learn that AI can create that end product for them, they shortcut right past the best part.

Let's build in opportunities for students to talk about the process—and show us their learning through it.

When AI cheapens the product, focus on the process.

## YOU'VE PASSED AI LITERACY 101: NOW KEEP IT GOING

Congratulations! Your AI literacy continues to grow. After reading these first few chapters, you have a better understanding of what the technology is and how it works. But this is only the beginning. Keep growing your AI literacy and learning about it by using it yourself. The more experience you have with the tools, the better you will understand their capabilities, their strengths and weaknesses, and how they should be used.

Now that you have a foundation of AI literacy in place, how can you help your students improve their own AI literacy—and support their learning in your class at the same time? We're just getting started. In the next chapter, you'll learn simple ways to incorporate AI awareness into day-to-day conversations. They're what I call "By the Way" Lessons—a quick, easy way to start integrating AI literacy into what you're already teaching.

## PROMPT AND PONDER

*To dive deeper into the contents of this chapter, personalize them, and reflect on them, take a picture of the prompt below. Upload the image to an AI assistant like ChatGPT or Google Gemini and simply say, "Let's do this."*

I am a teacher reading a book on AI literacy, and I'd like you to act as my personal AI literacy tutor. Your goal is to help me build my foundational understanding of AI in general and as it relates to the classroom. To start, please introduce yourself in a friendly, conversational tone and suggest three topics we could explore related to AI literacy essentials for educators. Some topics could include (but aren't limited to) how AI works, what to know about its results, data privacy and safety, best practices for using AI, concerns and dangers, etc. Tell me that I can choose one of those or provide a topic of my own. Once I make a selection, provide a concise, beginner-level lesson that explains the concept clearly, uses a relatable analogy, and highlights why it matters for my classroom or my students. Keep your explanation punchy and practical, avoiding overly academic jargon. End the lesson by asking if I have any follow-up questions, if there's a specific part I'd like to understand better, or if I'd like you to suggest three more topics to keep our lesson going.

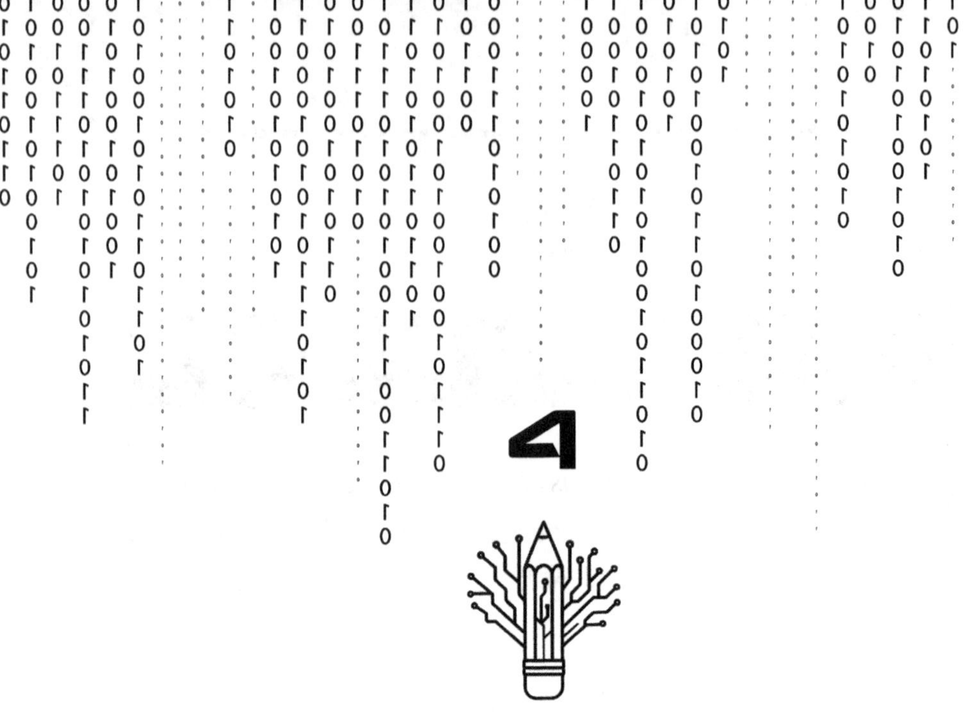

# 4

# SPRINKLING AI LITERACY INTO EVERYDAY CLASSROOM CONVERSATIONS

## MAKING "BY THE WAY" LESSONS PART OF YOUR DAILY CLASSROOM FLOW

In my Spanish classes, false cognates trick my students every time. False cognates are words that look alike in two languages but have distinctly different meanings. Some students grasp the concept quickly, but others continually struggle to remember that:

- *librería* isn't a library, it's a bookstore;
- *carpeta* doesn't mean "carpet," it means "folder";
- *pies* are feet, not delicious desserts;
- *sopa* is soup, not soap;
- *éxito* isn't the way out (the exit), it's "success" (which, technically, could be considered a way out); and
- *embarazada* does not mean "embarrassed"; it means "pregnant."

From day one in my Spanish classes, I am ready to offer a quick correction for any student who makes an assumption about a false cognate. In fact, by now, I have the correction memorized word-for-word:

"By the way, did you know that some words in Spanish look like words in English, but they mean something completely different? Those are called 'false cognates,' so you have to be careful!"

Two short sentences. But the impact can be huge.

I like to call these "By the Way" Lessons. These little nuggets of wisdom are brief, and teachers often start them by saying something like, "Oh, by the way, did you know?" If you're a teacher, you've probably used "By the Way" Lessons whether you realized it or not.

If we want to boost our students' AI literacy, it can start with small shifts just like this. It can fit in the context of our everyday classes and in the normal conversations we already have.

## MAKING A SMALL SHIFT IN WHAT WE ALREADY TEACH

Some people hear the term "AI literacy" and assume that we need to teach our students entire classes about artificial intelligence. Entire lessons. Special units.

Maybe.

But let's be honest. *Most* of us don't teach artificial intelligence. AI is not in our standards. We don't teach computer science. Instead, we teach specific subjects and grades like earth science, world history, fourth grade, music, speech, health, or physical education.

If someone is going to teach a whole class—or unit—on AI literacy, it's probably not going to be us.

But that doesn't mean that we don't see the writing on the wall. We see what's being predicted for the future of AI in our workforce and world. We want our students to be prepared—and we want to do something *(anything!)* to prepare them for that AI-integrated future. Even if we aren't the "tech teacher."

So ... what about us? What do we do?

Maybe a whole unit about AI doesn't fit in our curriculum and standards.

But two sentences about AI? A quick "By the Way" Lesson, 30 seconds long, about some nugget of wisdom related to AI? Yeah, we can make that fit into almost any lesson on any day.

This tiny shift is a big idea that I really believe in. We don't have to force a bunch of AI content and activities into our lesson plans to help students with AI literacy. But if we're willing to talk about it whenever it comes up naturally in class, we can teach students a little something about AI—and it can still support the curriculum, standards, and material we're supposed to cover in our classes. Plus, it helps students understand what's responsible and irresponsible, helpful and unhelpful, whether they're using AI in the way you asked them to—or they're using it on the sly when you don't even realize it.

This whole concept might seem small—teaching AI literacy two sentences at a time. But when students get little nuggets of wisdom throughout the week, throughout the grading period, the semester, or the school year? New nuggets of wisdom whenever they come up in discussion—and reinforcing old nuggets of wisdom from time to time? That persistence pays off. Eventually, teaching AI literacy two sentences at a time adds up to a practical, real-world education—on how real people are using AI responsibly (and not using it) and its implications on their work.

I've seen it in my own classroom.

I started to realize the importance of these "By the Way" Lessons at about the same time that I introduced my students to the picture of the pig and the sheep. (Do you remember that from the introduction?)

My students giggled at the AI-generated image of the two animals playing basketball against each other. We stopped to pick out all of the "AI weirdness"—the artifacts and oddities we observed that proved to us that it wasn't a true, genuine photo or illustration created by a human. After we spotted the AI weirdness, I sprung my first AI literacy "By the Way" Lesson on them.

"By the way, did you know that artificial intelligence makes these little mistakes sometimes? Looking for the weirdness—also known as artifacts—in an image is a quick and easy way to determine whether AI created the image or not."

Again, two short sentences. Not even a minute of instructional time. But the message was sent. My students had a better general understanding of how AI works and the impact it can have in their academic and personal lives.

Let's take a look at how we can insert little lessons about AI literacy into classroom conversations and lessons we're already having—and how it can even *strengthen* how we teach that curriculum.

## MASTERING THE SIMPLE "BY THE WAY" LESSON FRAMEWORK

To keep these short, punchy, and effective, I've been using the same framework to create these simple "By the Way" Lessons:

- Start the statement with: "By the way, did you know …"
- Give students one or two short facts about AI that relate to the topic or example at hand.
- Connect the new information about AI to whatever you're discussing so students see how it relates.

## "BY THE WAY" LESSONS

1. "By the way, did you know …"
2. One or two relevant, short facts about AI
3. Relate facts to whatever you're studying

For example: *"By the way, did you know that it's still valuable to practice writing even though AI is really good at it? Being a good writer is a skill you'll use your whole life. Plus, understanding how to write helps you determine if the response that AI gave you is quality or not."*

Of course, you don't have to use the words "by the way." There's nothing magical about those words. I've just found them an easy way to insert a quick tangent into a conversation.

## PRACTICAL EXAMPLES OF "BY THE WAY" LESSONS IN ACTION

Let's look at how these AI literacy "By the Way" Lessons might show up in actual classroom discussions. Let's start with a few deep-dive examples so you can see them in full context.

## AI OFTEN MAKES VISUAL MISTAKES IN IMAGES AND MEDIA

**Question:** By the way, did you know that artificial intelligence makes little mistakes in pictures sometimes?

**Context:** That weirdness is called an "artifact." Looking for artifacts in an image is a quick and easy way to help you determine whether AI created the image or not.

**What prompts this discussion:** When an AI model introduces "AI weirdness" (something that seems odd or unusual) in images, videos, or any form of media.

**Notes:** The AI models that make images (called "diffusion models") are making their best guess of what an image should look like based on patterns they've noticed in similar images. What they don't do, though, is count fingers, understand how normal human teeth look, or think about how many front seats a car should have.

**Discussion prompt:** What are other ways to spot AI-generated media? What happens when the models get better and it becomes harder to determine what is AI-generated?

## AI FREQUENTLY PRODUCES BIASED AND SLANTED RESPONSES

**Question:** By the way, did you know that AI sometimes produces biased responses?

**Context:** It learns from the data it receives from humans, and humans are biased. It passes on the biases it learns from us.

**What prompts this discussion:** When AI creates something that is overly slanted toward one perspective, one idea, or one demographic. You can also have this conversation when you see any type of content that is biased—even if it is human-generated.

**Notes:** AI does not just show bias based on sensitive subjects like gender, race, or religion. It has biases toward almost everything: vacation destinations, football offenses, and coffee roasts. If there is a range of opinions on a topic, AI probably exhibits a bias.

**Discussion prompt:** What are the other perspectives and people related to this topic that aren't reflected in the AI response? Why? How could we have approached this differently?

## AVOID ENTERING SENSITIVE PERSONAL INFORMATION INTO AI PROMPTS

**Question:** By the way, did you know that it's a bad idea to type your personal information into an AI prompt?

**Context:** If you type sensitive personal information—like your name, your bank account number, your telephone number—the AI model could deliver it to someone who could misuse it.

**What prompts this discussion:** When students type prompts that contain personally identifiable information (PII).

**Notes:** AI models—especially when you're using the free plan of an AI app—are not designed to keep sensitive information secure. Plus, even though sensitive personal information is not supposed to be used to train AI models, it could still fall into the wrong hands, especially if there is a data breach.

**Discussion prompt:** Why do you think people share their personal information with AI? How can you get what you're looking for without sharing that information?

Are you starting to get an idea of how these "By the Way" Lessons work? You start with a little wisdom about using AI responsibly. You add more context (if necessary) and connect it to your lesson.

In the examples above, you saw what prompts conversations like these, some additional background information about AI, and even a prompt to launch a classroom discussion with students about it.

## TEN QUICK AI TRUTHS FOR DAILY CLASSROOM CONVERSATIONS

Now that we know how they work, here's a list of ten quick "By the Way" Lessons about AI to share with students.

1. **By the way, did you know that AI makes mistakes?** They're called "hallucinations." Sometimes, if you tell an AI model it's wrong—even if it is actually wrong—it will insist it is right, so you have to be careful.

2. **By the way, did you know that ChatGPT is not always good at math?** It's a large language model, so it was developed to work mostly with words. (It has gotten better at math over time even though it was not designed for it.) When it has to process math, it sometimes struggles.

3. **By the way, did you know that discerning the line between "just enough AI" and "too much AI" can be difficult?** A good way to learn is to reflect on the outcome and try to improve next time.

4. **By the way, did you know that when you prompt an AI assistant, you don't have to get the prompt right the first time?** You can ask follow-up questions to get more detailed information.

5. **By the way, did you know that AI isn't human?** It sounds human. It uses the same kind of language that humans use. But it is actually a machine. Even though it sounds like us, it isn't a real person.

6. **By the way, did you know that there are times when we should disclose whether we've used AI?** This is called "transparency." If you've used AI to do a significant part of the work, others typically want to be informed.

7. **By the way, did you know that it's still important for us to learn even though AI exists?** Even though we can always ask AI for help, we still need to understand things for our day-to-day lives. Plus, we need to be able to determine whether AI-generated content is accurate or valuable.

8. **By the way, did you know that no matter your career path, AI will probably be a part of it?** Lots of employers are using AI to analyze data, brainstorm new ideas, and interact with others. The more you learn about AI now, the better prepared you'll be to understand and use it today—and in your future career.

9. **By the way, did you know that if you're not sure what AI can do to help, you can always ask it?** Just tell it what you're trying to accomplish and ask how it can help you. It will suggest some ideas for you to evaluate.

10. **By the way, did you know that AI makes its best guess at the right answer?** It takes vast amounts of data and makes a statistical guess based on what you ask it for. That's why it makes mistakes sometimes.

## PROMPT AND PONDER

*To dive deeper into the contents of this chapter, personalize them, and reflect on them, take a picture of the prompt below. Upload the image to an AI assistant like ChatGPT or Google Gemini and simply say, "Let's do this."*

I'm a teacher, and I want to use the idea of "By the Way" Lessons to help my students learn AI literacy through the lens of what we're learning in class. A "By the Way" Lesson is a quick little truth about responsible AI use that fits into the day-to-day conversations I'm already having in class. Here's an example: *By the way, did you know that AI makes mistakes? They're called "hallucinations." Sometimes, if you tell an AI model it's wrong—even if it is actually wrong—it will insist it is right, so you have to be careful.* Here's how I'd like for you to help. First, ask me what I teach and what my students are learning in class right now. Then, I'd like you to help me identify some natural places in my instruction where I could bring up important foundational understandings about AI literacy for my students. Be sure that they connect naturally to what I told you that we're learning in class. As you list these "By the Way" Lessons for me, I'd like you to also give me a bit of context about AI that will inform and guide me AND tell me the kind of conversations in class that might bring about that "By the Way" Lesson.

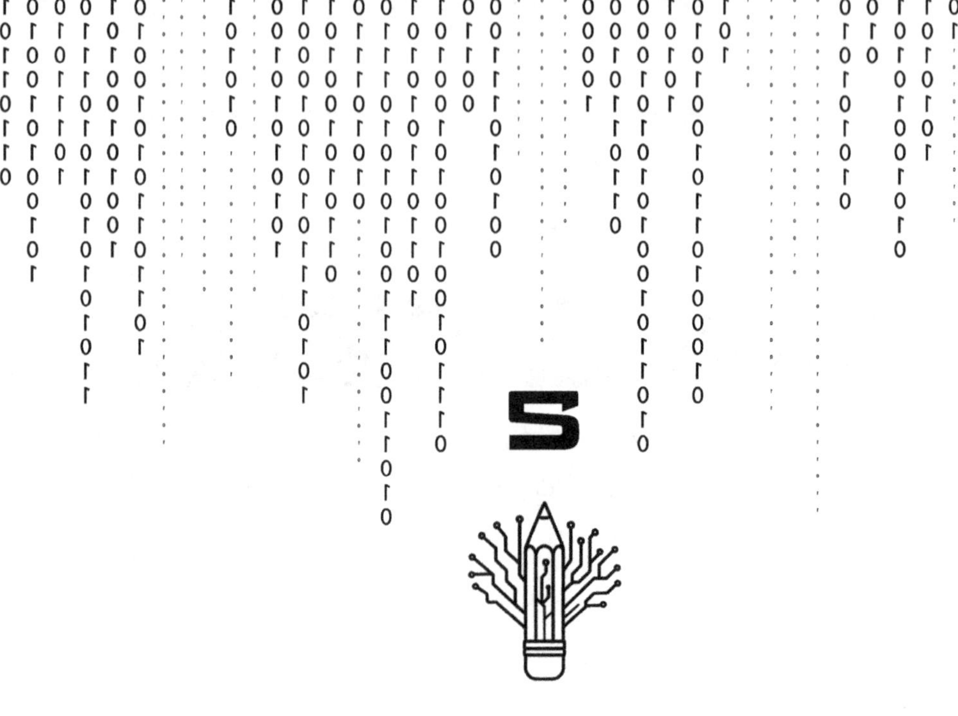

# 5

# LAYERING AI LITERACY ONTO THE CURRICULUM YOU ALREADY TEACH

## USING "BE THE BOT" ACTIVITIES TO AMPLIFY YOUR CURRENT LESSONS

You hear it from teachers of all grades and subject areas:

"I have so much to cover by the end of the year."

"We're only five weeks into the year, and I already feel behind."

"Oh great, there's a field trip today? I can't afford to have my students out of class for another day."

If you're a teacher, you know. The curriculum is always packed. The standards are numerous. There are always new initiatives and programs. And our list of responsibilities seems to grow endlessly.

And then here comes this guy writing a book called *AI Literacy in Any Class*, and it's easy to think, "Great, AI literacy. Yet another thing to add to my already full plate of expectations. I already have too much to do!"

But consider this ...

What if teaching AI literacy to students didn't actually add anything to your already full plate? What if, instead, it made it easier to clear that full plate? Could your students learn your class curriculum *and* AI literacy without it feeling extra?

I'm here to say: in many cases, yes. Adding an AI layer to what you already do can be a catalyst, amplifying your teaching and your students' AI literacy.

What does that look like? Let's examine one of my favorite examples of using AI to amplify what we're already learning. It's an activity called "Be the Bot." It uses an AI assistant, but it isn't an "AI lesson." It's still a lesson about your class content, but you use AI to push student thinking (and as something you can critique together later on).

## INTRODUCING THE "BE THE BOT" ACTIVITY

Imagine this: Your students have finished learning about a topic over the past couple of days—the Franco-Prussian War or mitosis or reading a chapter in the novel *Of Mice and Men*. They have some fundamental understanding of the material, and it's time to challenge them.

You say: "I am about to ask our AI assistant (large language model) a question about what we've been learning. But first, I want you to predict: how do you think it will answer?"

Then, you give the students the question. It's a bit of a subjective question, one that relies on some judgment or opinion, something they can defend. For example: Who were the three most pivotal people in the Franco-Prussian War?

The students get into small groups and brainstorm. Together, they make a list of possible individuals: Wilhelm I, Otto van Bismarck, Helmuth von Moltke, and Crown Prince Friedrich. But the answer can only include three people. Who makes the cut, and why?

The students finally narrow their answers down, and it's time for the big reveal. You type the question into your AI assistant—exactly as it was worded from the beginning. You hit enter.

The cursor blinks for a moment. Then, a cascade of words starts flowing onto the screen. You start slowly scrolling to reveal the AI assistant's response, and an audible buzz of student voices grows louder.

"Ah, see? I told you Wilhelm I was going to be first." "I knew it! We had all three of them." "Wait, how did Karl von Steinmetz not make the list? He was an army commander!"

This example of the "Be the Bot" activity is only getting started. There is so much more valuable critical thinking and conversation to follow.

But first, I have to ask you …

Is this a social studies activity? Or an AI literacy activity? I would argue that it's both, and I'd say it's more prominently a social studies activity.

To me, this is where AI literacy in the classroom is at its best—in the natural context of learning. The focus is still on the content, curriculum, standards, and the lesson of the day. But it pulls in valuable insights about AI that teach students about the very nature of artificial intelligence.

The best news? This is an activity that practically any teacher can use in virtually any content area or grade level.

Let's break down the "Be the Bot" activity to see how your students can use it to learn about your class content and AI literacy at the same time.

## PART ONE STARTS WITH A GOOD QUESTION

When you ask a good question, it piques students' curiosity and naturally motivates them to find the answer. Students explore concepts more deeply and gain a better understanding of how AI works—and how to use it more adeptly.

The question to avoid: a prompt with a clear, factual answer. You would not want to use: "In what year did the Franco-Prussian War start?"

Why? We ask AI assistants complex questions with ambiguous answers because we want to analyze the judgment calls they make. They don't have to provide a perfect answer. They just need to offer responses that we can critique. (In fact, when the AI provides flawed answers or judgment, it gives students even more to critique and judge.)

Some examples:

- **Elementary grades:** Who is the most courageous character in the book *Wonder*?
- **Math:** What are the most useful types of math in everyday life?
- **Science:** Which of these five environmental problems is the most urgent to solve?
- **Health:** What is the most important habit for a healthy lifestyle?

If you want to create your own "Be the Bot" questions, here are some of my favorite question starters:

- The best / most important / most influential
- Most likely to ...
- Choose one

- Make a recommendation
- Rank these items, events, or people
- Identify a turning point
- Who/what belongs in a group (categorization)
- The most / least ...
- Predict the outcome of ...

## PART TWO FOCUSES ON STUDENT BRAINSTORMING

Give students the question or prompt that you intend to ask the AI assistant. For example: "Who were the three most pivotal people in the Franco-Prussian War?"

This is where the activity becomes truly impactful. Here's why ...

**They begin "brain dumping":** "What are all of the possible responses the AI assistant could provide?" This is retrieval practice. Research shows that recalling information without the aid of notes or a textbook strengthens long-term memory. Even if they don't correctly predict what the AI assistant is going to say, they are already helping themselves to retain content for the future.

**They begin ranking:** "Of all the things we've just listed, what is the AI assistant most likely to say?" They use criteria to judge which item is best in the list. If you're using Webb's Depth of Knowledge as a framework for cognitive complexity, this shift immediately pushes the task to Level 2 (Skills and Concepts).

**They justify their rankings with evidence:** "OK, you've ranked your list, but how do you explain and defend it?" This is where the work becomes more complex—and remember, it's still based on the content your students are studying, rather than focusing solely on artificial intelligence. When students defend their rankings with evidence or even create their own rankings, it pushes the activity to Level 3 (Strategic Thinking) in Webb's Depth of Knowledge.

Notice the pedagogical shift here. Again, this is not strictly an "AI activity." In fact, you don't even need AI to complete any of these first steps. So far, what we've described could even be a traditional, non-digital learning activity.

However, to help your students develop AI literacy while strengthening their understanding of the lesson, this is when you introduce the AI assistant. It's time to submit the prompt and observe how the AI handles it.

## PART THREE LEADS TO A CLASS CRITIQUE

When I facilitate the "Be the Bot" activity with teachers at AI workshops, this is my favorite part. I submit the prompt we've all been considering, and the AI assistant starts slowly streaming words on the screen.

Why is this my favorite part? Because almost always, there's an audible buzz in the room. As the results appear, everyone immediately compares their own answers to the results the AI is generating. It's a slow reveal, and much like a reveal party, it's human nature to react when there's tension and the tension is resolved.

Instantly, whether I've asked them to or not, everyone in the room starts critiquing the AI results.

- **They notice alignment:** "Look! We had the same top three!"
- **They express surprise:** "Oh, that's a good idea. I didn't even consider that."
- **They defend their own logic:** "Hey, our number two response didn't even make the AI list! That's not right!"

This highlights an important aspect of AI literacy we'll examine more closely in the next chapter. That's the "ABC Rule," or Always Be Critiquing. We can critique this AI response based on what we've learned about the subject and the judgments we hold.

If we're going to critique the AI response well, we need two things: a solid understanding of the material we're studying and a basic understanding of AI. This is where AI literacy finally comes into play. When I run a "Be the Bot" activity,

I like to keep the focus on the content at first. But once those conversations start to wane, we analyze how the AI assistant handled the request. We start to ask:

- **What was the format of the response?** If it's a list, do you think it's a ranked list? (Did we ask it to rank the items?)
- **Are the responses any good?** How do we know if they're good or bad? How do we define "good" and "bad" in this context?
- **Is there anything missing or inaccurate?** Are any perspectives missing? Did the AI assistant's perspective lean in a certain direction? Was it biased? If not, what would it look like if it were biased? How do we know when it is biased?
- **Did the AI assistant respond the way we predicted?** How did we know to predict that response? What was unexpected?
- **What information do we think it used to respond?** What did we expect it to use? Is this different from how we would respond as humans?

The "Be the Bot" activity is a happy marriage between AI literacy and our curriculum. It gets students thinking critically. It provides substance for student discussion. Students analyze the AI responses to deepen their understanding of class content. And, by the end, you've provided opportunities to teach students the fundamentals of how AI works by showing them examples in context. (Plus, it's low-prep! When you're using AI as your teaching assistant, you may save a little time lesson planning and prepping for class.)

## EXPLORING MORE WAYS TO AMPLIFY STUDENT LEARNING

The "Be the Bot" activity is just one example of using AI to amplify what you already teach. (And thankfully, it's one you can incorporate into your lesson plans in virtually any subject area or grade level.)

Some teachers only use AI large language models (LLMs) like ChatGPT to generate lesson plans, worksheets, or grading rubrics. Instead, let's use it to help us do great teaching and learning—to facilitate the kind of learning activities that research says are extremely effective. (And let's use AI to help us complete that kind of learning in less time, with little or no prep work.)

Thankfully, when we engage in that kind of work, it provides an opportunity to examine the role that AI plays in the process. And when we do that, our students can learn foundational lessons about AI that help improve their AI literacy.

Here are more examples of AI literacy going hand in hand with class content. In all these examples, the teacher can put an AI assistant on the big screen in front of the class as a co-teacher—and to encourage class discussion.

These activities don't have to have the teacher lead the lesson from the front of the room. They can be student-centered, too. You can use AI chatbots that students interact with independently. That way, students are answering the questions and doing the thinking on their own. But if you're at a school where students don't interact with AI directly, you can also do the teacher-driven version.

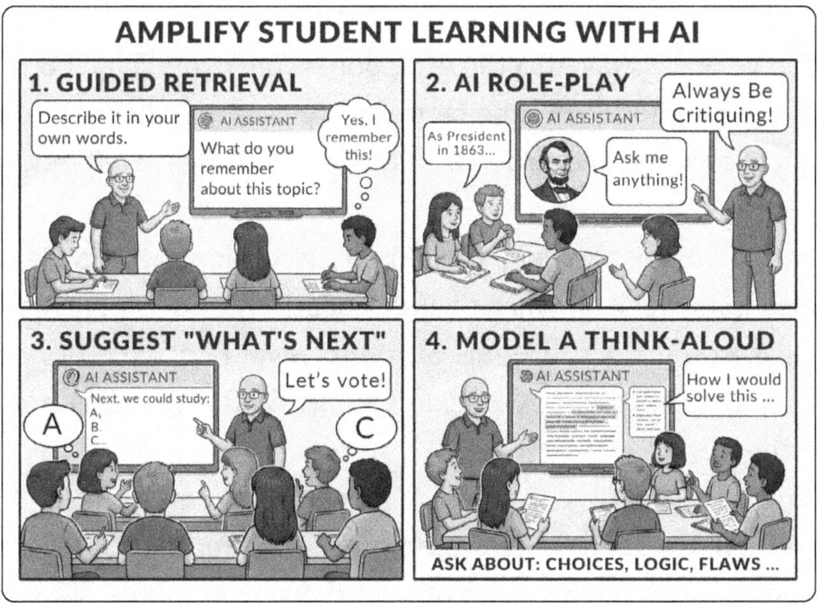

**Have AI create a "guided retrieval practice" session.** Ask it for recall prompts about what students are learning. Examples: "What do you remember about this?" and "Explain this in your own words." You can also ask the AI assistant to follow up with its own answers to those questions so students can analyze and judge them. Bonus: Ask AI to provide students with tips on how this retrieval practice works most effectively and how to use it better.

**Have AI play a role.** Use an AI assistant to speak in the voice of someone with a specific job, from a specific time period, or from a certain part of the world—or even in the voice of a character students have studied. The AI assistant can also role play job interviews and debates. Remember: Students should not assume that the AI responses are right! They should "always be critiquing" the facts that AI uses, the assumptions it makes in the background, and what it might have left out.

**Let AI suggest "what's next" in a discussion.** After a class discussion, ask AI what related questions or subtopics the class could pursue next. Students evaluate which ones they prefer, and they decide (alongside the teacher) how to proceed.

**Ask AI to personalize examples.** In a math lesson on percentages, have it generate word problems about sports, music, or hobbies your students care about. Let students give input and ask them to evaluate whether the AI suggestions are effective.

**Use AI to model a think-aloud.** Give it a reading passage or a text students are studying. Then ask it to narrate its reasoning or judgment process. How would it decide what is important? Students read its reasoning and lines of thought and then critique them: Did it make good choices? What did it miss? They might learn something they hadn't considered—or they might point out flaws in its logic.

Once again, none of these examples are "AI activities." AI isn't the main emphasis; your class curriculum is. Then, as an AI literacy bonus, we can analyze how the AI assistant handled certain tasks, what perspective it took, and how it organized its thinking. When we do that, we gain some valuable insight into how AI works (that's AI literacy), but we also get new and different insight into what we're learning.

## ELEVATING YOUR LESSONS WITH AN AI LAYER

Whether you're using a "Be the Bot" activity, another teaching strategy, or a different approach entirely, AI literacy can integrate seamlessly with what you need to teach.

View AI as a teaching assistant rather than just a tool for generating lesson plans, worksheets, or student feedback.

Treat AI as an additional layer—or a new lens—on the day's lesson to help students analyze and critique its output. Don't hesitate to be critical of the results, even if the critique is harsh. Remember, AI does not have feelings, so you can't hurt them!

AI literacy isn't about shielding students from flawed AI responses. Instead, it's about learning from AI's strengths while identifying and questioning AI's weaknesses.

## PROMPT AND PONDER

*To dive deeper into the contents of this chapter, personalize them, and reflect on them, take a picture of the prompt below. Upload the image to an AI assistant like ChatGPT or Google Gemini and simply say, "Let's do this."*

I am a teacher reading a book about AI literacy. I want to design a "Be the Bot" activity, where students predict an AI assistant's response to a subjective curriculum-based question and then compare and critique the AI's results against their own. I'd like you to help me plan this out. First, ask me what grade level and subject I teach, as well as the specific concept we are currently learning. Once I share that, act as an instructional coach to help me design the lesson. Please provide: (1) Three "Be the Bot" Prompts: Suggest three subjective, judgment-based questions I can ask an AI (e.g., "Who was the most pivotal figure in ..." or "Rank the most urgent environmental issues ...") that will spark a debate. (2) The Brainstorming Strategy: Give me a strategy for the student "brain dump" and justification phase to strengthen their retrieval and critical thinking. (3) The ABC (Always Be Critiquing) Guide: Identify specific elements of the AI's eventual response that my students should analyze, such as its internal logic, biases, or what it might have omitted. Ask your first question now so we can start designing this challenge together.

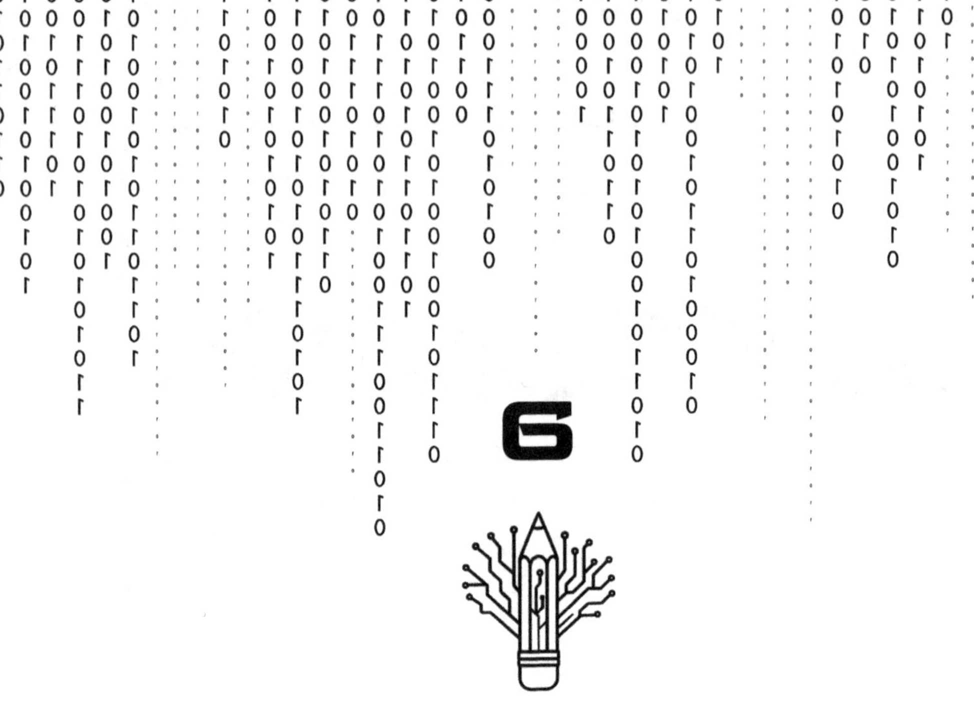

# 6

# CRITIQUING WITH CLARITY: IMPLEMENTING THE ABC RULE

## A PRACTICAL TOOL FOR EVALUATING EVERY AI INTERACTION

In sales, the "ABC" mantra is "always be closing." I want students—and teachers—to follow a different mantra whenever AI is present in the classroom. Always Be Critiquing.

Whenever AI is present—whether it is creating, responding, or analyzing—it always presents an opportunity for critique. That's because every time we prompt an AI model, behind the scenes, it has to make tons of judgment calls—calls we don't even realize it's making.

For example, if we ask it to write a sonnet about corgis (you know, those adorable, short-legged dogs), it must recognize the sonnet structure, extract the most pertinent information about the breed, determine how funny to make it, and make a judgment call on whether it's offensive to the corgi to talk about its short legs. (I don't think the corgis mind. They don't speak English, after all.)

This only scratches the surface. It might have gotten confused determining whether "Corgis" was someone's first name (rather than the plural form of the dog breed). It might have researched famous corgis worth mentioning in the poem.

When you use an AI large language model, we usually have no idea that all of this happens in the background when we ask for something innocuous like a dog sonnet. That's the problem: many people don't consider the various AI judgment calls happening in the background.

They also fail to consider ...

- What data is leading the AI model to reach that conclusion?
- How does the AI model's training influence the way the response is written?
- Is the AI response leaving out details or omitting people's perspectives?

Your students probably ask AI-powered apps all sorts of questions, receive recommendations, and ask for advice on lots of topics. But they don't consider how AI comes to a conclusion.

That demonstrates the need for AI literacy. Fortunately, there are many ways we can help students learn to evaluate and critique AI outputs—and the systems that create them. For example, they can examine:

- A summary written by AI of a book you're reading
- An AI analysis of a historical event you're studying
- An AI-generated image of a painting in a certain style
- An AI-suggested solution to a math problem

Help your students learn the basics of critiquing and analyzing artificial intelligence. You can help them critique both small and large outputs. Critique simple products like sentences and opinions. Critique the most complex AI models and their impacts on society. Critique it all. It's an AI literacy skill that will serve them well throughout their lives. Plus, it will help them strengthen their critique and analysis muscles in all walks of life—not just with AI.

Let's start using the "ABC Rule"—Always Be Critiquing—by identifying what our students can critique. Below are some examples and lessons that your students (and you!) might learn.

## ANALYZING THE PELOPONNESIAN WAR THROUGH A POP-CULTURE LENS

During my AI workshops for teachers, I have created numerous sample instructional materials as examples. At first, I wanted everything to be perfect—polished and flawless.

One time, AI created some seriously flawed text. I thought the lesson would be a disaster. But, to my surprise, the flawed text was more effective at teaching AI literacy than a perfect text. In this case, sloppy was better!

My prompt was: "Summarize the Peloponnesian War at an eighth-grade level, incorporating as many Taylor Swift song titles and lyrics as possible."

The results? Let's just say some of my students might call it "cringeworthy." Here's an excerpt:

*Picture this: Ancient Greece, sunshine, togas ... but hold on, things are about to go down like a bad breakup between BFFs. Enter Athens and Sparta, the two coolest city-states around. Athens, all about art, democracy, and "shaking it off" with their fancy navy. Sparta, the jocks with their strict military and "never getting back together" attitude.*

## IMPERFECT AI RESULTS OFTEN MAKE THE BEST TEACHING TOOLS

This "Taylor's version" summary was pretty bad. However, as I mentioned above, a product that's clunky and awkward can serve as a valuable teaching tool.

If we want students to think deeply about the curriculum *and* improve AI literacy, this "cringeworthy" summary actually works. When students analyze and discuss the AI work, they learn the content *and* better understand the inner workings of AI.

Consider these discussion prompts to analyze my "Taylor's version" example:

- Is the summary factually accurate? Are there any gray areas within these historical facts?
- Are the characterizations of Sparta and Athens fair? Would the Athenians or Spartans take exception to these descriptions?
- Does the inclusion of togas represent cultural stereotyping or a historical mix-up? (Spoiler alert: Togas were Roman; Greeks wore *chitons* or *himations*.)
- Encourage students to create a better version. Ask them to write their own short summary of the Peloponnesian War using song titles or lyrics from Taylor Swift or another artist, then identify and defend their choices.

When AI creates imperfect results, it can create a more powerful teaching moment than a polished, perfect response. Students notice the imperfections, oddities, and errors in judgment. They begin to realize that AI is fallible; it makes mistakes, lacks nuance, and mischaracterizes. When they see these errors, they make an important connection: "If AI screwed up there, think of the errors it might make in other places!" In essence, exposing students to imperfect AI-generated content teaches them AI literacy while strengthening their overall critical thinking skills.

## IDENTIFYING SUBTLE BIASES IN EVERYDAY AI RECOMMENDATIONS

I'm a self-proclaimed coffee snob. I can buy and drink coffee from a fast food restaurant, a gas station, or even (gasp) Starbucks! But that doesn't mean that I have to enjoy it. Thanks to friends like Dee Lanier, Ken Shelton, and Scott Nunes, I have learned to appreciate quality coffee roasts and single-origin coffees from all over the world. I'm a sucker for light roast Ethiopian and Colombian coffees, and I experienced some phenomenal coffee while visiting Costa Rica.

So, naturally, upon learning about the capabilities of large language models, I asked Google Gemini to recommend the best coffees for home brewing. I hoped to discover hidden gems that I hadn't noticed before.

Nope. I was highly unimpressed.

The AI suggested Peet's Coffee French Roast, Death Wish Coffee Dark Roast, Illy Classico Coffee Medium Roast, Cafe Bustelo Coffee Espresso, and Starbucks Coffee Pike Place Roast (yuck).

As my lip curled in disgust, I noticed several distinct patterns in the list. First, the recommendations were all major coffee chains—coffees available at most supermarkets in the United States.

Second, I noticed that every recommendation was either a medium or dark roast.

It appeared that Google Gemini exhibited a bias against my beloved light-roast coffees.

## AI BIAS EXISTS IN EVERY POSSIBLE SUBJECT MATTER

Discussions on AI bias often focus on categories that spark intense debate, such as gender, race, culture, or politics. These biases show up in blatant ways sometimes, and we should always be ready to critique them. But we also should be ready to critique the AI bias that shows up in more subtle ways. Examples: how AI ranks its results or which perspectives it prioritizes in the background. Sometimes we don't see these leanings on the surface, but if we keep prompting and keep analyzing, it often reveals them.

When AI bias shows up in controversial topics, those will always dominate the headlines. But AI shows bias on virtually any subject. I observed it in coffee recommendations. But you might also see it in suggestions for:

- Book genres, where thrillers and romances often overshadow poetry and historical fiction.
- Football offenses, where the pass-heavy NFL might influence an AI model's suggestions.
- Travel destinations, where popular coastal spots could overshadow less common locations.
- Music preferences, as rock and pop dominate AI training data and can skew results.
- Nutrition and diet, which often reflect Western perspectives and what's available at grocery stores.

Regardless of the subject matter, AI-generated content will inevitably reflect certain biases. Encourage students to challenge those biases by asking questions like ...

- What kind of data probably dominates the training data? And how does that data probably influence the results?
- Whose perspective is prioritized in these results, and whose is marginalized?
- What is a counterargument or differing perspective to the one the AI provided?

## SIMULATING CONVERSATIONS WITH CHARACTERS FROM LITERATURE AND HISTORY

Once teachers realized what AI large language models could actually do, one of their first ways to use it creatively was to simulate conversations with characters in history and literature. (I mentioned this briefly in the previous chapter.) They simulated the historical figures students study, characters from novels they read, or people with a certain career—even people who lived in a different part of the world or have totally different life experiences. In my Spanish class, my students have chatted with fictional characters to practice their conversation skills. In teacher workshops, I ask participants to engage with chatbots simulating figures from history, like Theodore Roosevelt, George Washington Carver, and Cleopatra.

Depending on the tool and the prompt, sometimes the experience is great—interesting, revealing, and fun. But when it's not, the simulation feels superficial, forced, and, at times, inaccurate and inappropriate.

Some educators really push back against using these fictional character interactions for a variety of reasons (some I'll share below). I get it, and I think we should tread cautiously when we use them. But in the end, we have to understand a key AI literacy component about these simulated AI conversations: These are not real people. We simply don't know for sure if what the AI is saying is actually what those people would have said. As long as we keep that in mind, these simulated conversations are just more AI content we can analyze and critique.

## SIMULATED AI CONVERSATIONS ARE SIMPLY CREATIVE WRITING EXERCISES

When AI plays a role, it's all just a creative writing exercise for the machine. The AI model isn't actually becoming these people; it's just guessing. Sometimes, it can get a little carried away trying to replicate them.

If we keep the right perspective, these chats can start some great discussions. After an AI simulation, students can analyze and critique it by asking:

- Were the facts the AI provided accurate?
- Did the character say anything they wouldn't have known—like modern language or slang, new inventions, or recent historical happenings? (These are called "anachronisms.")
- Is there anything the character actually wrote or said in real life that tells us how they might really respond—and does it line up with the AI response?
- What do we know about the person's time period and location—and how might that impact their perspective? Was the character similar to or different from others living at the same time?

- Is the AI model perpetuating stereotypes that are debunked, unfair, or simply inaccurate?

These character chats can be fuel for analytical and critical discussions. Students shouldn't use them as core, factual information. (Unless the students do some extra digging to ensure that the AI wasn't just making it up).

Why? Because when we ask AI to be creative, it tends to play fast and loose with the facts to make the story better. (In fact, that's a part of AI literacy that students can take with them: the more creative the request, the further the AI might wander from the truth.)

There's a more dangerous side to all of this. Sometimes, students (especially younger ones) have a hard time knowing whether they're talking to a real person or not. The line blurs between fact and fiction, between reality and fantasy. It's easy to see why. When humans text message other humans, the user interface in the app looks exactly like a chat with artificial intelligence. The context clues start to fade. It becomes harder and harder to tell whether the app they're using is powered by AI or a human, especially for young children.

And when students start to confuse an AI model for a human being, they're putting their trust in an unpredictable system that lures people into unhealthy AI relationships, suggests dangerous choices, and gives bad advice.

Language is incredibly powerful. We humans use language to convey emotion and connect with others. AI uses that same language, but to the model, it's just completing a task. Words may be neutral to a machine. But to humans, words are meaningful. They impact us psychologically and can cause us to do unwise things if we lose track of what's real and what's artificial. We need to teach students to be on their guard and to simply avoid situations where they might be manipulated by AI.

## PRACTICAL STRATEGIES FOR IMPLEMENTING THE ABC RULE

We've just covered three examples where students can strengthen their critique skills. Now, let's look at a versatile framework we can use to help students analyze AI outputs. Below are some practical steps you can take to help students become critical AI evaluators—so they better understand the logic behind the scenes with AI and the impact it has on humans.

## START THE CONVERSATION WITH STRAIGHTFORWARD QUESTIONS

First, you need something to analyze. It could be a sample of AI-generated text in the style of a writer you're studying, an AI-generated image of a historical event, an AI explanation of a math solution, or even an AI-generated alternate ending to a story your class has read. Give AI a task to do that aligns with what students are studying.

After students examine the output, several straightforward prompts can spark a discussion:

- What do you think: is this effective?
- Could you tell that the content is AI-generated? How?
- Is there anything that's out of place or just "not right"?
- What do you see? What do you notice? What do you wonder?

Note: When students respond to questions like these, the teacher doesn't need to provide every "right answer" to their observations. Remember, the goal is to get students thinking and noticing. We want them to analyze and critique. They don't need the teacher to respond or answer their questions perfectly. In fact, when a teacher is brave enough to say, "I don't know either," that could be the best outcome. It could lead students to investigate and solve their own questions.

## ANALYZE AI CONTENT FROM SMALL TO BIG—OR BIG TO SMALL

When I look at something AI-generated through an analytical or critical lens, I tend to find something medium-sized.

By that, I mean that I tend to overlook tiny details right away. And I often tend to overlook the big picture, too—how all of the details are working together in harmony (or working in opposition!). There's a good chance that your students might analyze and critique in the same fashion.

If you want to broaden your AI critique conversation, I encourage you to go smaller—or to go bigger. Move between specific details and overarching themes. Use the AI critique bullseye chart as a guide.

At the center of the chart are the narrow details of your content. The outer edges are the big-picture, overarching parts. In your discussion with students, figure out where you are on the chart and then go narrower or broader.

For example, when analyzing an image, you could ask questions about one single detail in that image. Then, pull it back more broadly: does the composition of the image work as a whole? Even broader is the overarching message that the elements and the composition are conveying. And the most expansive level of all is the cultural influence and impact that similar messages are making. Move from specific to general, or vice versa—whichever works best.

Here are some other ways to critique AI, moving from specific to general:

- **In writing:** from word choice (specific) to sentence structure, paragraph organization, and an overall analysis of the complete work (general).
- **When discussing impact:** how it relates to an individual person (specific), peer groups, the local community, and society (general).
- **In decisions:** a specific thought (specific) turns into an action, which leads to an outcome, and finally creates (or fails to create) a paradigm shift (general).

Of course, these aren't the only ways you can move between narrow and broad perspectives. If you want a custom idea for whatever your students are studying or discussing, take a photo of the bullseye chart (yes, you have my permission) and upload it to an AI large language model. Then say: "Using this chart as an example, give me some examples of how we could analyze [your subject] from big to small."

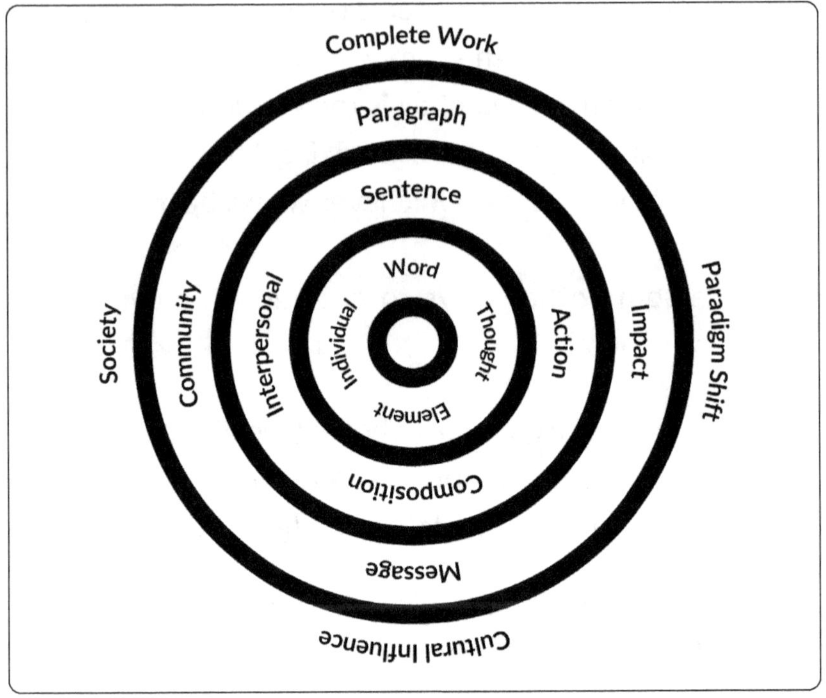


## PUT ON SOMEONE ELSE'S SHOES TO EVALUATE AI OUTPUTS

Our personal perspective naturally colors how we see, interpret, and evaluate our world. How would someone else see a situation differently? How might they react?

AI can mimic someone's perspective if we ask. But, often, we don't ask. If we don't specify a perspective, it must make internal algorithmic choices behind the scenes. Those assumptions show up in its responses. Ask students to identify whose worldview the AI response best reflects—and whose voice is missing.

Putting on someone else's shoes can completely shift the context of a topic. We can ask our AI assistant to provide a response from the perspective of someone with a different background, a different upbringing, or a different occupation. This shift shows how much that perspective influences the information that AI provides.

Predicting AI bias before hitting enter is a fantastic way to engage students. Have them guess which viewpoints the model will prioritize, then run the prompt and compare the actual results to your students' predictions. As an extension, ask the AI to justify the assumptions it made and the perspectives it chose so students can critique its logic.

## BUILDING BETTER THINKERS THROUGH CONSTANT AI CRITIQUE

Is all of this talk about critique and analysis just about AI literacy? Not at all.

In fact, these skills will strengthen your students' overall reasoning and logic. As you integrate these habits, you will likely see these skills grow in every subject. Students will be able to apply this scrutiny to a variety of fields—and they'll be able to lean on these critical thinking skills in discussions and solve problems in their everyday lives.

See? These AI literacy skills don't just teach students about technology; they build better thinkers. When we adopt the "ABC Rule" (Always Be Critiquing), evaluation and critique become expected parts of working with AI. Students notice when AI exhibits flawed reasoning or inconsistent logic. They learn to question and verify before accepting AI-generated work as accurate.

They realize that AI isn't always right. It's never truly neutral. Every output leans toward a specific perspective or opinion. There are always internal decisions being made in the background. If students learn to interrogate and critique AI outputs, they will be more aware of those leanings and can act accordingly.

## PROMPT AND PONDER

*To dive deeper into the contents of this chapter, personalize them, and reflect on them, take a picture of the prompt below. Upload the image to an AI assistant like ChatGPT or Google Gemini and simply say, "Let's do this."*

I am a teacher reading a book on AI literacy for the classroom. I want to apply the ABC Rule (Always Be Critiquing) by finding specific AI-generated work for my students to analyze and evaluate. I'd like you to help me identify the best "artifacts" for us to critique. First, ask me what grade level and subject I teach, and what specific topic my students are studying right now. Once I respond, act as an instructional designer and suggest three distinct types of AI-generated work related to that lesson that would be perfect for student critique. For each suggestion, explain: (1) The Artifact: What specifically should I ask the AI to create (e.g., a specific type of summary, a role-play transcript, a math explanation, or an image prompt)? (2) The Hidden Judgment Call: What is a likely "internal decision" the AI will have to make that my students should look for? (3) The Critique Question: One high-impact question my students can use to evaluate the quality or bias of that specific piece of work. Ask your first question now so we can start curating these critique-ready materials.

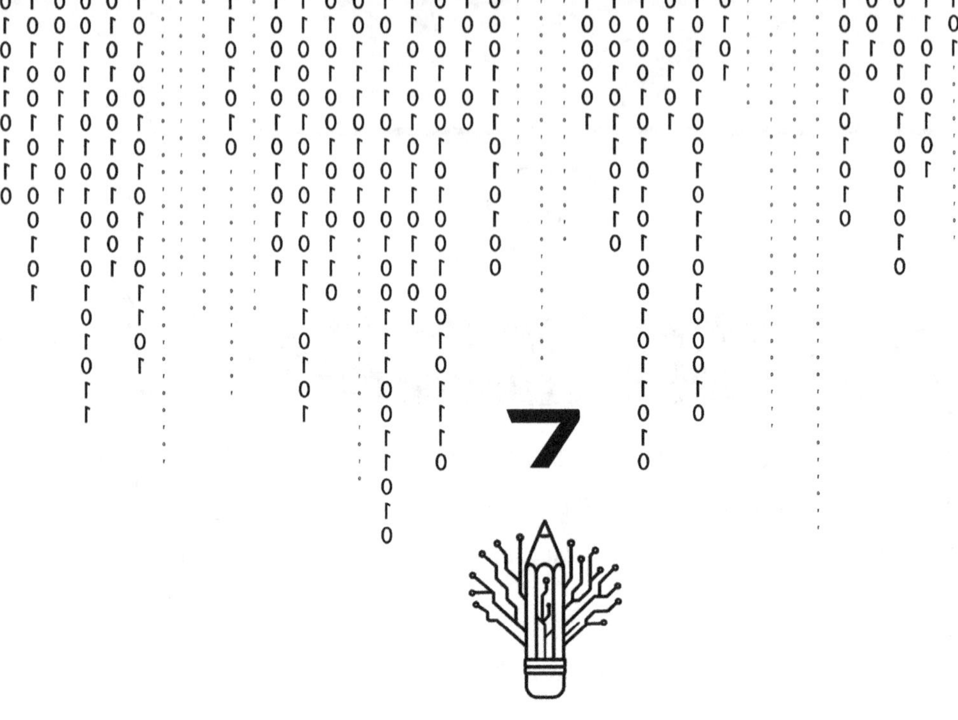

# 7

# ANALYZING YOUR LESSONS THROUGH AN AI JUDGMENT LENS

## CONNECTING CLASSROOM CONTENT TO REAL-WORLD AI DILEMMAS

Artificial intelligence will likely have a significant impact on many sectors of the workforce, government, daily routines, and the global landscape. We can explore these implications within many topics students study at school.

Here's an example. In high school social studies or government classes, teachers often discuss international conflicts and how governments resolve them. When these disputes escalate into war, nations navigate wartime scenarios differently.

## ANALYZING ETHICAL DILEMMAS WITH AUTONOMOUS MILITARY DRONES

**Consider the rise of autonomous military drones.** Equipped with advanced AI computer vision, these drones can travel long distances to identify and neutralize enemy targets using lethal force. The use of these autonomous systems raises ethical questions:

- Should we allow artificial intelligence models to identify enemy targets?
- If AI identifies a target, should the system be allowed to use lethal force without human input or approval?

- If we insist on human approval—which requires more time—what happens if we face an adversary that does not, creating a tactical disadvantage and a potential loss of life?
- Given that AI-powered computer vision models often struggle to accurately identify individuals with darker skin tones, how much trust should we place in those systems?
- Since these drones protect human soldiers from direct danger, should that advantage be weighed in our ethical analysis?

The ethics of applying AI in this scenario could spark a compelling discussion in a social studies or government class. But this isn't just for social studies class. The ethics of using AI can be discussed in lots of classes, subject areas, and topics—and it can lead students to better understand the curriculum and content they're learning.

## DEBATING OWNERSHIP AND ETHICS IN AI-GENERATED ART

**Consider the ethical implications of AI-generated visual art.** AI image generators, powered by diffusion models, learn how to create imagery by studying millions of pieces of art. Then, using a simple text prompt, they create art in any style to illustrate nearly any concept. In short, they mimic human creation in ways that are sometimes imperceptible to the average eye.

People who use AI image generators love getting access to free, customized, high-quality visuals. However, to the artists whose work was used for training the AI models, it often feels like large-scale piracy or plagiarism.

This technology raises some serious ethical questions, such as:

- Should AI systems be permitted to create imagery in a specific artist's style?
- Should a system be allowed to generate art in a style that's not exactly the same but similar, in what some might consider a remix, a derivative, or a form of "fair use"?
- Is it ethically responsible (or reprehensible) for an AI company to harvest images by scraping the internet to train their AI models?
- Should the general public feel uneasy about using these tools? Is there a moral obligation to refuse them entirely?
- What about the gray areas? What if an aspiring artist uses an image generator to create inspiration before creating a final piece by hand? What if an artist uses AI to remix a work so significantly that it becomes transformative? At what point is one crossing the line?

The ethics of using AI generators can create rich discussion in art, philosophy, or classes exploring legal precedents.

These conversations are AI literacy lessons. But they're also social studies and government lessons. They're art, philosophy, and law lessons. Every academic discipline offers logical entry points for ethical questions, fairness debates, and practical AI applications.

That's the essence of embedded AI literacy—and the broader impact of AI on our world. It's coming for everybody. AI technology may eventually reshape nearly every profession, business model, and daily routine in our personal and professional lives.

To prepare students for this future, we should not study artificial intelligence in isolation. We do not need more canned units and lessons about machine learning or computer science in a vacuum. We need to see these tools applied in practice, within specific contexts. Then, we must be able to discuss ethics, determine how to responsibly proceed, and critically analyze competing viewpoints. That helps our students—and all of us as human beings—better prepare to act in a logical, responsible manner when the situation requires it.

(Students can also learn a lot by analyzing the implications of artificial intelligence on their classwork, too, but we'll explore that in a future chapter!)

## CONNECTING AI LITERACY TO STANDARD SUBJECT AREAS

We can use an AI literacy lens to discuss with students topics they are already studying. Students can learn the curriculum *and* broaden their AI literacy at the same time.

I've found that there's a simple, natural progression guiding these discussions:

1. Students master basic concepts about a topic.
2. Students examine how AI influences situations, relationships, and dynamics in that topic.
3. Students observe, identify patterns, and ask questions.
4. Students make judgment calls and evaluate the reasoning of others, justifying their own conclusions.

This applies across the K-12 spectrum, from the littles (early elementary) to the bigs (high school) and beyond. Let's look at some examples along with key concepts and questions that students can analyze.

## A SCIENCE DISCUSSION ABOUT BIOMES

### KEY CONCEPTS TO EXPLORE:

- AI systems rely on massive data centers to train expansive models.
- These processes consume significant amounts of electricity and water.
- Data centers often consume billions of gallons of water that local ecosystems depend on. Plus, when water is used to cool AI systems, it is frequently returned to the source at higher temperatures (thermal pollution), potentially disrupting the surrounding environment.
- The electricity required by these AI models can contribute to pollution and a substantial carbon footprint.

### DISCUSSION QUESTIONS:

- Where does the water go when data centers use it—and how does this impact biodiversity?

- If you don't want a data center in your biome or ecosystem, is it OK to move it to a different biome or ecosystem? Who would it impact? Who gets to decide?
- When technological advancement conflicts with environmental preservation, how should we determine the best course of action?

## A MATH DISCUSSION ABOUT STATISTICAL PREDICTIONS

### KEY CONCEPTS TO EXPLORE:

- AI becomes "artificially intelligent" by processing vast datasets—text, images, and records.
- That information is never truly neutral. Because it's derived from human activity, it inevitably contains biases and leans disproportionately in certain directions.
- If the data underrepresents or overrepresents a person or an idea, the AI results will reflect that imbalance.
- These types of statistical predictions power systems such as facial recognition, hiring algorithms, medical diagnostic tools, and credit approvals.

**DISCUSSION QUESTIONS:**

- If AI is consistently less accurate for one group than another, how might that affect people's lives?
- How should people navigate using AI to make important decisions if they know that the underlying data is likely biased?
- How can AI developers use better data? What defines "better data"? What are the potential challenges in acquiring it?

## A HEALTH CLASS DISCUSSION ABOUT GETTING HELP

**KEY CONCEPTS TO EXPLORE:**

- AI large language models will provide a response to almost any inquiry.
- People sometimes seek medical advice or mental health support from AI models that they would typically reserve for a healthcare professional.
- AI does its best job to provide helpful responses, but it can suffer from poor judgment or provide inaccurate information.

- This is particularly dangerous when discussing sensitive topics, like mental health or specific medical treatments.

**DISCUSSION QUESTIONS:**

- What are some other topics that could pose a safety risk if discussed only with AI assistants?
- How can you tell if your interaction with an AI is crossing into unhealthy or unreliable territory?
- What if someone lacks access to healthcare professionals? Is it better to get advice from AI than receive no guidance at all? How do you manage that risk?

## A PRIMARY GRADES DISCUSSION ABOUT COMMUNITY HELPERS

**KEY CONCEPTS TO EXPLORE:**

- Artificial intelligence (can be framed as "the computer" in primary grades) helps our community helpers every day.

- For example, doctors and nurses use computers to check our health, rescue workers find lost people with drones, and farmers tend their crops with machinery.
- Since computers sometimes make mistakes, human helpers are always there to catch them.
- When computers and people work together, they can do more—but we still have to be careful.

## DISCUSSION QUESTIONS:

- How do computers help our community helpers?
- How can our community helpers make sure the computers aren't making mistakes?
- What's something you'd like a computer to help someone do?

## PROMPT AND PONDER

*To dive deeper into this concept, upload images of the above examples to an AI assistant and use the prompt below:*

I am a teacher. I like how the examples in these photos connect core curriculum with AI literacy. I am about to teach [subject or concept]. Using these photos as a guide, create a comprehensive plan to teach this topic through an AI literacy lens. First, ask me questions to understand my specific needs. Then, create a custom guide for incorporating AI concepts and conversations into my lessons, matching the style of the examples provided.

## APPLYING ETHICS AND JUDGMENT LENSES TO INSTRUCTION

It's easy to look at our curriculum and think, "How in the world does AI literacy even connect to this?" The reality is that AI literacy is more than understanding AI systems and how to use them.

AI literacy is rooted in judgment and ethics—navigating tricky areas where right and wrong aren't clearly defined. For students, the best way to understand these nuances is to discuss them, wrestle with them, and explore "wrong" answers to eventually find the right answers.

Judgment and ethics aren't just AI literacy issues. They're vital to critical thinking. They help students understand complex issues deeply through debate and persuasion. In short, they're the types of learning practices that transform students into thinkers.

We can add an ethics and judgment lens to almost any lesson, and it will support AI literacy, whether the conversation mentions artificial intelligence or not.

**Judgment and ethics conversations (with an AI literacy angle):** These help students see the unique twist AI puts on real-world issues within the subject they are studying.

**Judgment and ethics conversations (without an AI literacy**

**angle):** These build students' general analytical skills. They naturally spot AI literacy issues because they are already skilled at identifying ethical dilemmas in other disciplines.

We can apply these ethics and judgment lenses to almost any topic students study or discuss. They can be adapted for younger students and older students and help us critique, judge, and act fairly. When we strengthen these skills, students become more adept at making responsible decisions—regardless of whether AI is involved.

1. **An integrity lens:** How do we handle this responsibly? Who gets to decide what responsibility looks like? How might various perspectives differ on what is considered responsible? **AI Literacy Angle:** At what point does AI assistance stop being "your own work"?

2. **A fairness lens:** What is fair? How do you know what's fair? Is this cheating? If so, how can you tell that it's cheating? Is anyone left at a disadvantage? Does anyone gain an unfair advantage? **AI Literacy Angle:** If AI algorithms favor specific voices or outcomes, when does it become unfair—and how can we address it?

3. **A practicality lens:** Could this be made more practical or more helpful? In what ways is it actually doable? Are there ways in which it isn't doable? **AI Literacy Angle:** Which AI promises are actually practical? Which are simply hype?

4. **A humanity lens:** How does this highlight the human touch? Does a human's perspective or role make this outcome better or worse? Is this a task that only a human should be trusted with? **AI Literacy Angle:** What elements of human connection are lost when we turn to AI for support?

5. **A learning lens:** How does this help a human improve their skills and understanding? What do humans stand to benefit from completing this task themselves? **AI Literacy Angle:** Does using AI in this specific way deepen our understanding, or does it bypass the struggle needed for growth?

6. **A safety lens:** Could this put anyone at risk? How big of a risk is it? Is there a danger in doing nothing? How much risk are we willing to accept? **AI Literacy Angle:** How do we protect our digital and physical safety – and is there danger in ignorance or inaction?

7. **An appropriateness lens:** Does this behavior align with civil and appropriate standards? Are there boundaries we are willing to cross for specific reasons? **AI Literacy Angle:** If we incorporate AI into this process, are there social or moral boundaries we are crossing?

8. **A perspective lens:** Is one viewpoint overrepresented? Is anyone's perspective left out or marginalized? **AI Literacy Angle:** Which voices has AI amplified, and which has it minimized?

9. **A transparency lens:** Is the process or background clear? Do we know the steps that lead to the results we are analyzing, or is the creator hiding important details? **AI Literacy Angle:** Should we disclose how much AI was used in a work – and should we know how the AI reached its conclusions?

10. **A creativity lens:** What is the source of this creativity? Did the creator develop the idea themselves, or did they use an outside source for inspiration? Does external help make it less of a creative work? **AI Literacy Angle:** How much AI assistance can a person use before a work is no longer considered "human creativity"?

11. **An autonomy lens:** Who or what is in control? Is the control where we think it is, or is there manipulation happening behind the scenes? **AI Literacy Angle:** How does artificial intelligence shape choice, independence, and agency—and who really holds the power?

12. **A trust lens:** How is trust earned in this situation? Is our trust earned through evidence, or is it just implicit? Could someone or something mislead us? What would be the implications of that? **AI Literacy Angle:** How much trust do AI systems or AI outputs deserve—and why?

13. **An efficiency lens:** Does improving efficiency cost us something important? Could this be changed to be more streamlined? How do we define "efficient" in this context? **AI Literacy Angle:** What do we gain or lose when we turn to artificial intelligence for efficiency?

14. **A consent lens:** Do those that are participating understand what the implications are? Is there anything misleading or unclear about their participation that could have a negative impact? **AI Literacy Angle:** What does consent mean in a digital world—from data collection to facial recognition to AI art models trained on human creators' work?

15. **An empathy lens:** Are we accurately considering the emotions and situations of others? Are there assumptions we've made that might be wrong? How might an incorrect assumption cause harm? **AI Literacy Angle:** How should we use technology that can only simulate, rather than feel, human emotion?

## DEVELOPING AI LITERACY THROUGH ONGOING CLASSROOM DISCUSSION

AI literacy is more than a single unit or lesson delivered once a year in a technology class. It has implications for every subject in all grade levels. It impacts virtually every topic we teach—and virtually any lesson that students learn.

When we view our curriculum through an AI literacy lens, students gain a deeper understanding of both artificial intelligence and the material they're learning. That leads to enlightening discussion and helps students to see how their skills apply to real-world situations.

In these situations, AI literacy is no longer "just something else added to my plate." It reinforces the important concepts students must learn while preparing them for an AI-driven future.

## PROMPT AND PONDER

*To dive deeper into the contents of this chapter, personalize them, and reflect on them, take a picture of the prompt below. Upload the image to an AI assistant like ChatGPT or Google Gemini and simply say, "Let's do this."*

o I'm a teacher reading a book about AI literacy in the classroom. Act as an educational coach and AI literacy expert to help me explore how the rise of artificial intelligence impacts both my teaching and my students' lifelong learning habits. Begin by asking me about my specific job, the subjects I teach, and the age group of my students. Once I provide that context, guide me through a structured yet encouraging conversation exploring several key themes and how they apply to my personal educator assignment: Personalized Learning, Finding Balance, Human Uniqueness, Responsible Modeling, Shortcut Psychology, Sparking Curiosity, and any other related and relevant topics. For each area, explain the concept briefly and ask how it might manifest in my specific classroom or curriculum.

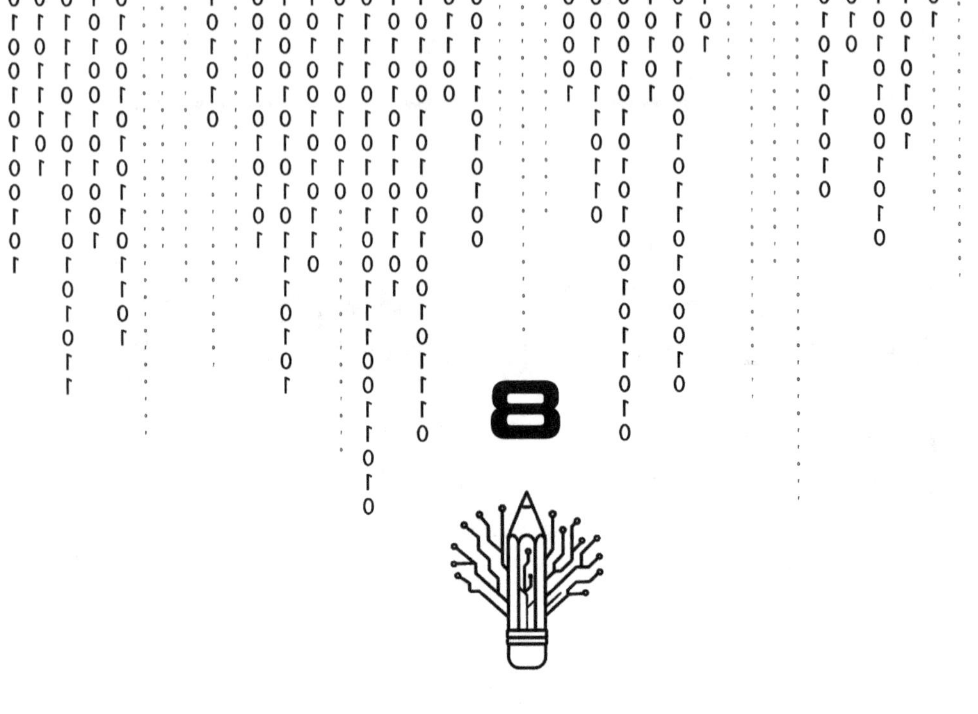

# 8

# BALANCING THE BOTS WITH THE BEST OF BEING HUMAN

## CENTERING CONNECTION AND CHARACTER IN A DIGITAL WORLD

A school district I worked with recently surveyed parents about their feelings about AI in education. The results were fascinating and wide-ranging, but they captured the heart of the concerns many of us share.

The parents worried that AI would stunt problem-solving skills and diminish critical and creative thinking. I have to admit: as a parent myself, I share these same concerns!

This tension is central to AI literacy for our students. In an AI age, how do we keep learning going? How do we grow as human beings? How do we choose which tasks to handle ourselves and which to delegate to AI so we don't lose what's special about our humanity?

These implications on learning are also implications on life if we look at them the right way. They're about living what we'd call "a good life" and doing things "the right way." The more students learn about that while they're still in school, the better they can thrive and maximize their human potential when they graduate and enter the "real world."

How do we teach in a way that keeps learning active so AI doesn't derail it? And how do we help our students become lifelong learners in a future where AI can handle most of the thinking and problem-solving for them?

What is the role of education when all the world's information is at our fingertips and capable AI models can explain concepts and help us transform that data?

Let's examine that. Here are some implications AI has on learning (and life) to think about as we plan lessons and design activities—and discuss with our students so they're thinking about them, too.

## THINK ABOUT THE POWER OF PERSONALIZATION

If you talk about the impact of AI on education long enough, someone will inevitably mention "personalization." For decades, education has often been a one-size-fits-all experience—and if you've ever tried it on, you know that one-size-fits-all clothing usually fits no one. In seconds, a well-crafted prompt can provide specific strategies for individualizing instruction.

For teachers, AI helps us connect curriculum to students' interests, like their goals, dreams, and aspirations—or their favorite snacks, bands, and apps. Many AI platforms provide data on student performance, highlighting specific challenges, collective class progress, and next steps. This data can help us make more informed instructional decisions.

It can do the same for students. A student can quickly ask an AI assistant to explain a concept using an analogy from their own world — whether that involves football, culinary arts, or classic fables. They can connect content to their goals or a future career, helping to answer that age-old question: "How will I use this in the real world?" Or they can even make it entertaining: "Explain this new concept like a comedy sketch by my favorite comedian."

This ability to personalize goes beyond the classroom, too. When students see how to apply these tools to learning, they recognize how AI can generate tailored suggestions for their personal projects and interactions with others.

There's a caveat, though. It's a lesson I learned from my friend, education leader Ken Shelton: "Sure, you can personalize ... but you have to know the person!" At the core of personalization is still the individual. We have to prioritize empathy and relationships. Without that human connection, AI-driven personalization becomes hollow and superficial.

## THINK ABOUT THE DELICATE ACT OF BALANCE

Managing the balance between AI and humanity is delicate work we will navigate for the rest of our lives—especially our students. How much AI use is too much, and how much is not enough? Often, when we discuss this balance, we get caught up in sweeping generalizations.

- "I hate AI."
- "Oh, AI is the best!"
- "You should always (or never) use it."
- "Using it like this is always right (or always wrong)."

Use AI too much? Connection, empathy, and human-to-human understanding suffer. We lose the fundamental human elements that matter most.

But use AI too little? We run the risk of wasting time on tedious tasks—and missing out on new, helpful ideas.

It's a balancing act, and when we get it right—as students, as teachers, as humans—it makes us feel truly human.

- We lean on it lightly when our own capacities benefit from a little support.

- We delegate heavily to AI on tasks where we want to preserve our human attention for what matters most.

School is a fantastic proving ground to help students understand how to manage this balance. Whether we realize it or not, students are making difficult judgment calls on whether to use AI or their limited human attention every single day. (More on that in the next chapter.)

Let's help students analyze how AI could be used in a variety of life situations—and whether it's right or wrong. Let's help them determine how it should and shouldn't be used in classwork to ensure they are acting ethically and responsibly.

The more practice students get at navigating that balance, the better equipped they will be when they transition to higher education, the workforce, and their adult lives.

## THINK ABOUT THE UNIQUENESS OF HUMAN THINKING

Human thinking is unique. We each perceive the world based on our life experiences, education, personalities, and cultural viewpoints. No one else interprets the world exactly the way you do—or I do.

AI definitely doesn't see the world the way that humans do. It has its own superpowers: the ability to analyze immense datasets in seconds to provide us with useful outputs, such as text, imagery, and code.

But AI doesn't really know what it's like to smell an apple pie in a warm kitchen. It doesn't know how it feels when a toddler runs to you with their arms outstretched. It doesn't know the impact of heartache, love, loss, or pride on the human heart. It doesn't understand the impact of our relationships on other humans. AI has no way of perceiving it, so it can't account for these nuances in the work it does for us.

Human thinking isn't just unique. It defines our humanity. We must be ready to use what makes us special and fiercely guard against AI overstepping there.

But still, sometimes, we give away our opportunity for deep human thinking by letting AI think for us. All of us—students, teachers, all human beings—must be cautious about delegating the tasks and qualities that make us special. Sometimes, we outsource to AI so we can focus on what matters. Other times, we sacrifice our opportunity to be ourselves—to be truly known—simply to save time.

But when we have to trade what makes us special, what are we really saving? And is that trade ever truly worth it?

## THINK ABOUT MODELING RESPONSIBLE AI USE

Many people operate on vibes and gut feelings without evidence to back them up. There is lots of skepticism about AI, and many are acting on their emotions with little to no experience or data.

If you know something about AI and have improved your AI literacy, **you're in the minority.**

If you have actually experimented with AI in a variety of scenarios and decided how it helps or hinders, **you're in the minority.**

If you have analyzed the impact of AI use in your own work—and how it could impact others—**you're in the minority.**

When you're in this minority, modeling becomes crucial. You have the opportunity—and the responsibility—to show your students how they should approach their work when it comes to AI. You can do this by modeling what you have learned and explaining your reasons for each decision.

- **Modeling is important for teachers because of their position of authority.** When they show students how and when you use AI personally—and why you choose not to—it provides a blueprint to follow. (Some won't follow it, but some will!)
- **Modeling is equally powerful for students.** When students engage with AI responsibly, they can transform an entire school culture. If a student sees a classmate using AI in a productive, unique way, they might re-evaluate how they use it. If enough of them change, they're all modeling appropriate use—and that's how culture evolves.

- **Modeling is important in the workplace, too.** Employees, much like students, reinforce culture when they approach their work differently and justify their decisions with sound judgment.

Right now, too many people dismiss AI as fundamentally harmful—and they won't do their homework to defend their beliefs. Once you've improved your AI literacy, you have a perspective that uninformed critics don't.

Make up your mind based on evidence. Stand your ground, and be willing to talk about it.

## THINK ABOUT THE PSYCHOLOGY OF TAKING SHORTCUTS

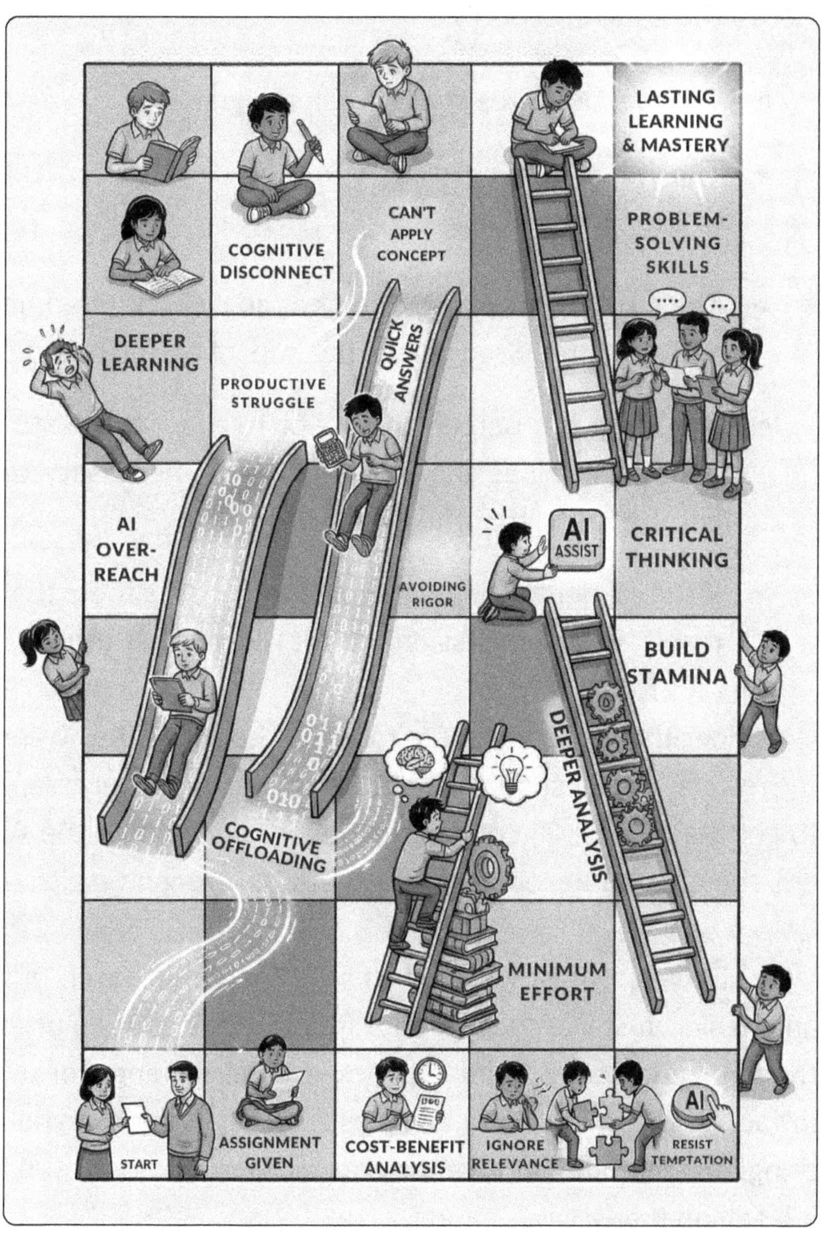

We have struggled with shortcuts in education for decades. The workplace has, too.

Here's the issue in schools:

- The teacher gives students an assignment.
- The student doesn't see the relevance in the content or the task.
- The student does a cost-benefit analysis of the time and effort required versus the impact on their grade.
- Based on the perceived lack of relevance, the student determines the minimum effort necessary to get the result that they need.
- If the student can find a shortcut that gets them that result with even less effort, they'll consider using it.

Why does the student want to take the shortcut? They want the results. They just don't want to exert the effort necessary to get the results. Of course, the deeper we get into the AI era, the easier it becomes to shortcut effort to get results.

Why? Because AI is designed to be a "people pleaser." It's an enabler. Just like social media, it's designed to keep us in the app—and keep us coming back—by doing things for us. In fact, sometimes I'll tell an AI assistant *not* to do certain things for me but just give me suggestions and ideas—and it'll still do it anyway.

As educators, we know that cognitive struggle is essential for lasting learning. But it is, by definition, a struggle, and it's human nature to avoid a struggle. If students can find a way to skip the struggle—even if they understand that struggle is good for us—they are tempted to take it. (It's like telling me that there are peanut butter cups in the pantry and not to touch them!)

An important part of AI literacy is recognizing that AI wants to do the work for us, and we must be able to resist.

- Keep focused on your goals and the reason why you're avoiding the AI shortcut.
- Use self-discipline. Follow through on your word when you're tempted to shortcut with AI.
- Build up stamina to endure work and struggle over time so you won't wear down. This means choosing what will make us better humans until it becomes a repeatable habit.

As teachers, when we notice that students are making smart choices and building that stamina, we can praise and encourage them. Remind them of the value of the struggle—beforehand as a warning, during the task as a reminder, and afterward as a celebration.

As humans, when we understand the "why" behind our efforts, we're less likely to take shortcuts and miss out on the whole reason we're doing it in the first place.

## THINK ABOUT THE SPARK OF STUDENT CURIOSITY

Movies with a predictable ending are the worst. (OK, there are probably other types of movies that are worse, but just go with me on this.)

You're watching the movie and there's some sort of tension or conflict. Immediately, you think, "I know what's going to happen next!" Then you spend the next hour or two (or more!) watching everything unfold exactly the way you expected.

For students, learning can be like a movie with a predictable ending. No conflict. No tension. No unexpected plot twists. Similarly, adult life can start to feel like a movie with a predictable ending. You get stuck in the same old rut—same job, same routine, same locations, all the same.

Curiosity can provide plot twists. It can provide us with an adventure—a journey that we never expected to take with twists and turns that bring us some excitement.

How does this apply to AI literacy? An AI assistant is like a rollercoaster of curiosity and excitement just waiting for you to sit down, buckle up, and take off. As soon as you encounter an unsolved mystery (whether small or enormous), embrace it. Grab your phone (or laptop), open your AI assistant, and start asking questions. If you're like me, you'll get in a flow state where you lose track of time and space around you.

It's fantastic.

If you're a teacher, I encourage you to help your students lean into curiosity whenever and however you can. It's electric. In the AI age, you're no longer expected to have answers to all of your students' curiosity questions.

It's like the slogan at an AI event I attended at Google headquarters once stated: "The future belongs to the curious." Curiosity can supercharge learning. It might be the spark that ignites a lifelong burning fire of passion for your students.

## LIVING THE GOOD LIFE THROUGH AI LITERACY

I'm hoping you didn't read that subheading as "AI gives us the good life." (Hopefully, by now, you don't see me as an uncritical AI cheerleader.)

I believe that AI literacy helps us live a more intentional human life—a real, true human life that's full of the best of humanity. AI will continue to integrate into more parts of our lives. If we don't pay attention, we risk subconsciously handing over the best parts of being human to the bots.

AI literacy is about understanding AI. Seeing where it is. Knowing when it's influencing us. Then taking control of the influence and control we let it have in our lives. When we do that, we maximize our humanity. We live life.

Granted, this chapter was a little more philosophical than the others. But the ideas in it—personalization, balance, human thinking, modeling, avoiding shortcuts, and curiosity—are the glue we need in the daily routine of the classroom. Hopefully, these are a compass to help us navigate this rapidly changing landscape.

## PROMPT AND PONDER

*To dive deeper into the contents of this chapter, personalize them, and reflect on them, take a picture of the prompt below. Upload the image to an AI assistant like ChatGPT or Google Gemini and simply say, "Let's do this."*

I'm a teacher reading a book about AI literacy in the classroom. Act as an educational coach and AI literacy expert to help me explore how the rise of artificial intelligence impacts both my teaching and my students' lifelong learning habits. Begin by asking me about my specific job, the subjects I teach, and the age group of my students. Once I provide that context, guide me through a structured yet encouraging conversation exploring several key themes and how they apply to my personal educator assignment: Personalized Learning, Finding Balance, Human Uniqueness, Responsible Modeling, Shortcut Psychology, Sparking Curiosity, and any other related and relevant topics. For each area, explain the concept briefly and ask how it might manifest in my specific classroom or curriculum. If I am unsure how a concept applies or feel stuck, gently and encouragingly suggest practical examples for me to consider, such as how to balance AI efficiency with human empathy or how to turn an AI shortcut into a moment of productive cognitive struggle. Throughout our dialogue, focus on how I can model intentionality so that students learn to use AI as a tool for growth rather than a replacement for human thinking, ultimately helping them navigate a "good" life where curiosity and deep effort are protected and celebrated.

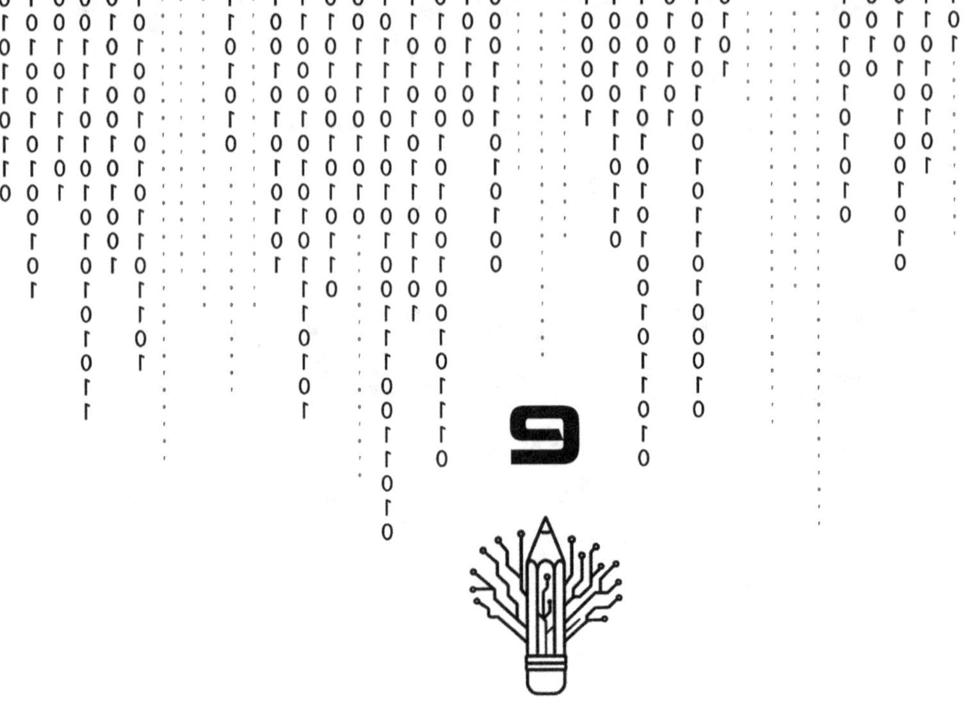

# 9

# AI AND CHEATING: BUILDING A CULTURE OF ACADEMIC INTEGRITY

## MOVING FROM POLICING TO PARTNERING WITH YOUR STUDENTS

"What about cheating?" In staff meetings. In the teacher's lounge. On social media. When discussing AI with educators, the topic of conversation inevitably comes back to cheating.

I get it. Teachers see this challenge daily and struggle to manage it (myself included).

**Here's the problem: there's no simple, universal solution.**

- We quickly discovered that the most obvious response—block it or ban it—doesn't actually work.
- Students can use AI tools on personal devices at home or smartphones at school to do classwork.
- Teachers have tried AI detectors, but they're wildly inaccurate—and are only looking for blatant copy/paste AI use in student work.
- Relying on AI detectors leads to false positives, creating unnecessary confrontations with students who actually did the work and are accused of cheating.

If you have experienced this, you know how you feel. Helpless. You feel like you've lost control. If students bypass the learning and thinking, then we start to wonder: why are we here in the first place?

Here's the reality, though: we're not alone.

## RECOGNIZING OUR SHARED STRUGGLE WITH AI AND INTEGRITY

This isn't just happening in schools. It's all over the workforce. Employees everywhere are testing the boundaries of AI in their professional work, and it's causing all levels of business to make hard AI judgment calls.

**For employees,** AI causes some to be more productive than ever. They might think: "AI is making me look like a workhorse! I can't believe this is making me money." Or they might wonder: "Is this too far? Am I using AI too much? What if my boss finds out and thinks I'm overusing AI?"

**And the boss?** The boss notices the shift in productivity and begins to question the value of human labor, asking: "How much human thought is actually happening right now? Why am I paying for work an AI can do? Do I really need to employ humans?"

**Meanwhile, the company** adopts AI too aggressively and the product suffers. Eventually, someone notices, whether it's the employees, the supervisors, or worse—the customers.

This is also being felt in creative circles like the art community.

**Some creators refuse to let AI compromise their work**—and sneer at others who use it at all.

**Some creators use AI in every stage of their work**—seeing it not as art, but as a means to generate a sellable product.

**Many creators sit somewhere in the middle,** using a blend of human skill and AI support—but finding the right balance is a challenge.

The classroom reflects the same tension we see across society. What's the right balance between AI input and human contribution? What do we lose if we get the balance wrong?

Like I said: we're not alone.

## BUILDING AN OPEN AND TRANSPARENT CULTURE AROUND AI

This isn't an "anti-AI cheating" chapter. You won't find tips to make your class AI-resistant or AI-proof. This is a book about AI literacy—the skills and knowledge necessary to navigate a world full of artificial intelligence.

Here's what this chapter is all about. Academic integrity issues are windows into real-life choices students will make in their future careers. They provide a vital opportunity to discuss the balance and right relationship between AI and humans.

When we talk about AI and cheating in the open, it helps students consider when to lean on AI to support their work and when to leave AI out—and what domains should remain human-only.

It's tempting to try to just banish anything AI-related. If you've thought about it, I hear you. I have, too. We all feel the allure of getting rid of the messiness that AI brings to the classroom.

However, we have to embrace these two realities:

1. We can't eliminate it. We just can't.

2. We can help students to think differently about their AI use.

By bringing these topics into the open, we help students understand what's at stake—and what happens when they misuse or overuse AI.

When we normalize the presence of AI rather than treating it as a taboo secret, here's what happens:

- AI is no longer something students whisper about when teachers aren't around—or use in secret to "get away with something."
- Students start to see examples of how AI can be used responsibly to support learning and to help them grow as people.
- They recognize that there's a choice when they do their work—both with benefits and consequences.
- They're challenged to consider the implications of AI overuse, asking themselves: "What kind of person do I want to be?"

Here's what fascinates me. These conversations make students more mindful of how AI impacts their learning. Cheating might actually decrease, not because teachers are catching it more, but because students want to act with integrity. They want to be responsible. When they see AI used responsibly—and see their classmates acting responsibly, too—they'll feel empowered to make better choices. These habits become a foundation they carry into higher education and their professional lives.

Now, I understand that what you just read sounds incredibly optimistic. Will this healthy AI culture fix all cheating problems? Absolutely not. Cheating has existed as long as formal education. It comes in all forms: cheat sheets, glancing at other students' tests, copying a friend's homework. AI is just the latest—and perhaps most tempting—tool for bypassing the work. However, technology isn't the root cause that students cheat. Cheating is a symptom of deeper problems in education that have existed for ages: irrelevance, toxic grading culture, motivation, disconnection from personal goals, lack of time, lack of sleep, and even disrespect. As the classic Billy Joel lyric suggests, "We didn't start the fire." These issues were burning long before AI entered the equation. Now that AI is here, we need to have these AI literacy conversations about academic integrity. We can talk about and model the appropriate use (or non-use) of AI in everyday classwork.

## CO-CREATING A SHARED PATH TO ACADEMIC INTEGRITY

At the beginning of the year, some teachers will give stern warnings about consequences. They might say: "Don't use AI to do your work. That's cheating! If I catch you using AI, you'll receive a zero and be written up."

This approach immediately creates a rigid, top-down power dynamic. It suggests a "do as I say" mentality: "I'm the boss whether you like it or not. My rules are final, and I don't need to hear what you think about it."

Regardless of whether the teacher deserves that level of authority, it sets up an adversarial relationship in the student's mind. Student vs. teacher. Once established, this dynamic can lead to a year-long struggle unless it's intentionally dismantled.

It doesn't have to be this way.

Instead, let's invite students to co-create their own norms and guidelines for using AI in classwork. Many students already have a keen sense of what's fair, of what's right and wrong. (Plus, they're even more confident when they get to judge the fairness of someone else's actions!) We can use that to our advantage.

Start at the beginning of the school year, semester, or grading period. Or if you want to start now, there's no time like the present.

Consider discussing some of these situations with your students. (Note: These conversations can be brief if there's minimal AI influence on your classwork or span multiple days if there's significant AI impact.)

## STEP 1: A DISCUSSION ABOUT AI IN PROFESSIONAL FIELDS

AI integrity and fairness aren't just a classroom issue (as we previously discussed). In lots of professions and areas of life, creators and professionals (as well as responsible human beings) are struggling with the human/AI balance. Start by discussing those implications.

Warning: If you immediately start by talking about classwork and the impact of AI, students might want to do what's in their own best interest. ("Let's answer in a way that makes less work—and easier work—for us.") But if you start by discussing the impact of AI on other areas of life, they're more likely to judge impartially rather than focusing on whether this will make their own assignments easier or harder.

**Example: Artists.** At one end of the spectrum, you *can* create art with AI using minimal human effort. But should you? What are the implications? At the other end of the spectrum, some artists avoid all AI technology. Does it matter, and if so, why? Between those two extremes is a blend of human skill and AI assistance. At what point is a work no longer considered human-created? How can we tell?

Other examples:

- **Writers and journalists:** When does AI support their writing—and when does it create inauthenticity and misinformation?
- **Healthcare:** How far should AI go to help a doctor diagnose and treat diseases and injuries?
- **Customer service:** AI customer service can save time and money. But it can also create a poor customer experience. How do you balance this?
- **Law and judges:** Could AI make judgments more fair—or do the human lawyers and judges serve an important role that AI can't fill?
- **Leaders and managers:** If AI can help with hiring decisions, job promotions, and disciplinary actions, how much power should we give AI?

**Resource:** Want more specific examples in a certain field or your content area? Just tell an AI assistant app about the conversation you want to lead, give some of these examples as a guide, and ask for some examples specific to your content area or field.

A robust discussion with students about these topics will create a natural transition to a conversation about classwork because the issues are so similar.

## STEP 2: A DISCUSSION ABOUT AI IN ACADEMIC TASKS

Students often grapple with the balance between relying too heavily on AI and missing the support it can give their learning. The students already feel that tension. Teachers worry that discussing AI will "open Pandora's Box," showing their students how to use AI inappropriately. But let's be honest. Most already know. And if somehow they don't, then a small dose of prevention can be better than a truckload of intervention.

**Example: Essays.** On one end of the spectrum, students could use AI to generate an entire draft. But what do they lose in the process? Why would students do that? (This conversation can be uncomfortable, but the student's perspective can be really revealing.) On the other end of the spectrum, students could completely avoid AI and the internet and technology all together. This approach has benefits and drawbacks. Ask students about them. In the middle of the spectrum, scattered between those extremes, is AI assistance. How do we know when AI assistance is appropriate—and overreach? Are there times when one way of using AI is *appropriate support* for some students—and *overreach* for others? How do you judge that?

**Other examples:**

- **Science labs:** When does AI help students interpret data—and when does it jump to the conclusion before students process it?

- **Math equations:** When does AI help students check their work—and when does it solve the problem before they've learned anything? How can we strike the right balance?
- **World language translation:** When does AI provide a quick word or phrase to support communication—and when does it stand in the way of building language skills?
- **Reading comprehension:** When does AI help students understand a text more deeply—and when does it interpret and make meaning for the student?
- **Social studies analysis:** When does AI provide new viewpoints for the student to consider—and when does it provide full observations the student doesn't have to think about?

**Resource:** The "AI Writing Spectrum" graphic. I created this visual to help teachers and students have productive conversations about responsible AI use. Visit **ditch.link/aispectrum** to download a PDF that can help facilitate conversations.

After these classroom-specific conversations, students have a better idea of what's at stake and what the implications are. This sets the stage beautifully for them to help set their own class norms and expectations around AI use.

## STEP 3: A FRAMEWORK FOR SETTING SHARED CLASS NORMS

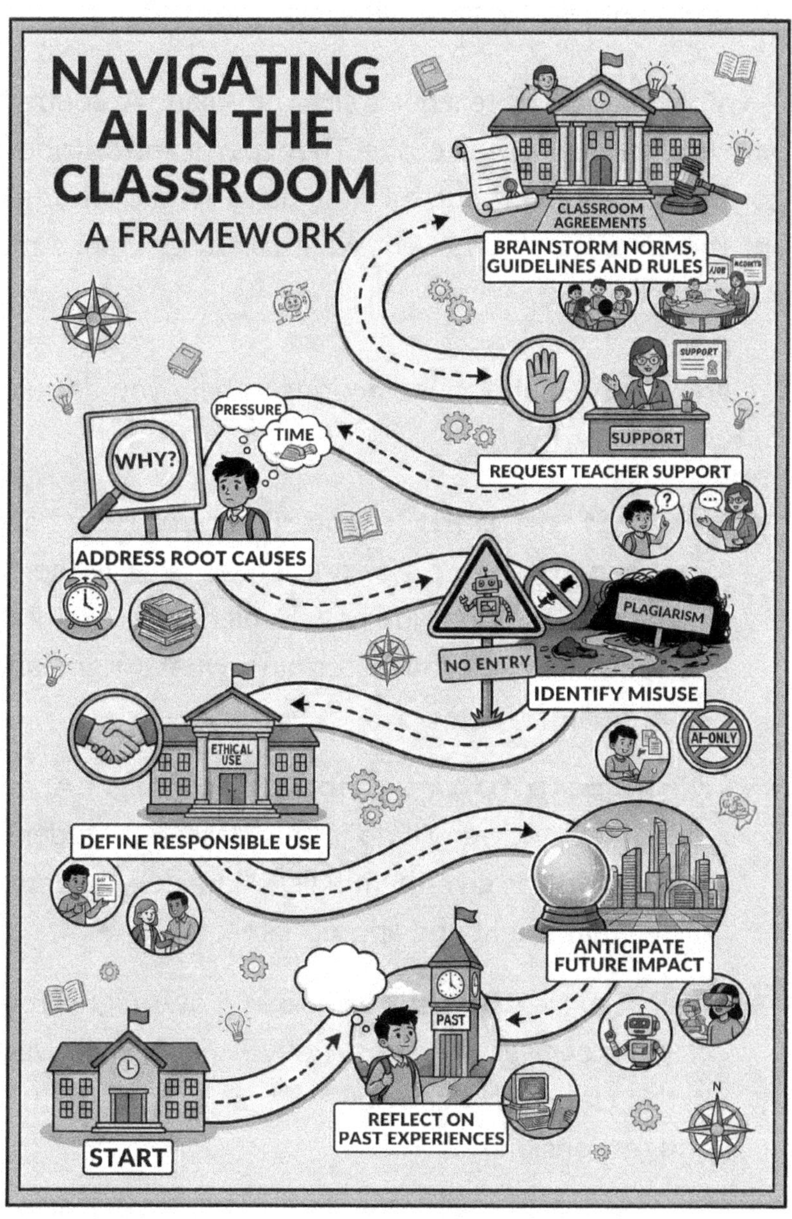

Sometimes, teachers provide a list of AI do's and don'ts to students at the beginning of the year. The problem with that? Students don't have any ownership. They don't understand the restrictions, so there's often a lack of buy-in.

(Also problematic: The teacher grabs a pre-made AI contract from a teacher resources website. They copy it and distribute it to the students without thinking about what role they want the contract to serve—or what role they want AI to serve in their class.)

Here are some questions and actions to help you develop a culture of integrity:

- **Reflect on past experiences:** How have you seen AI impact classwork in the past? Give some examples—and describe how it might be harmful or helpful. How do you determine what's right and appropriate?
- **Anticipate future impact:** How might AI impact the work we will do in this class? Let students brainstorm—or give them a list. How do you determine what's right and appropriate?
- **Define responsible use:** How might your classmates use AI in constructive, responsible ways in this class? How can you tell that it's constructive and responsible?

- **Identify misuse:** How might your classmates misuse AI—in this class or in other classes? How do we know that it's irresponsible?
- **Address root causes:** When students overuse AI to bypass thinking, what are the real reasons? Is it lack of motivation? Irrelevance? Thinking that they can't do the work? Not truly understanding what they're supposed to do? Lack of time?
- **Request teacher support:** What can your teacher do to reduce the temptation to use AI irresponsibly? What support might you ask of your teacher, and is it reasonable?
- **Brainstorm norms, guidelines and rules:** What would be fair? What would help us to learn and grow?
    - **Norms** state how we do our work and state: "This is how we do things here."
    - **Guidelines** are practical suggestions: "Here's a good way to approach this."
    - **Rules** are non-negotiable requirements: "You cannot cross this line."

Determine together where specific scenarios require rules versus guidelines. Discuss where exceptions might exist and how to handle judgment calls to ensure fairness.

Establish a protocol for "ambiguous territory." What should a student do if they are unsure about a specific use of AI? How should they proceed to maintain their integrity?

Then, discuss accountability. How should the teacher address a situation where AI overreach is suspected? By agreeing on the enforcement process ahead of time, you remove the "student vs. teacher" friction by working together to come to a fair solution.

After some discussion, come to some conclusions about how you and your students will handle academic work in an AI-capable world. Depending on your classroom culture, consider signing an agreement or displaying them where everyone can see.

## NAVIGATING THE MESSY DAILY REALITY OF INTEGRITY

Once those norms, guidelines, and rules are in place, that's where the real AI literacy work begins. Before, students were discussing the appropriate place of AI in their classwork in theory. But when they start working on classwork, it's time to actually put those discussions into practice.

This implementation phase is complicated and hard. Trust me: when you help students navigate these messy situations, this is where the real learning and the real change happens.

Don't avoid it. Pull on your rubber boots and wade through the mud and the muck with them.

As students start doing real classwork with these norms, guidelines, and rules in place, you'll probably see several student archetypes:

- Many students appreciate clear expectations and actually feel safer with guardrails in place (whether they tell you or not).
- Others will test the norms, guidelines, and rules by bending them (without breaking them). However, they will still try to abide by them.
- Some students will still over-rely on AI to bypass thinking and hard work.

Teachers are in a tricky spot because we can't actually see whether students are using AI irresponsibly. When you watch students work—or ask them about their work, it can be hard to discern whether they're using it to support thinking or skip thinking. Plus, modern AI models produce such natural human language that it's hard to distinguish from human work.

For now, the eyes of a human teacher—and their intuition—will give us clues when students' work is inauthentic. When this does happen, it provides opportunities for AI literacy conversations. (Remember, this isn't the book to bust AI cheaters or to make your lessons AI-proof!)

Teachers are using a variety of strategies to address these moments:

- **Some have face-to-face discussions.** They're showing students what they've noticed and why they believe the work to be inauthentic.
- **Some utilize student check-ins.** They're asking students to explain their understanding of content and their reasoning behind their answers.
- **Despite being notoriously unreliable, some teachers still rely on AI detectors.** Unfortunately, AI detectors reduce the conversation to a binary "did you use it or not?" which frames AI usage as a simple "cheat/no-cheat" scenario. That dynamic will cause some students to do whatever it takes not to be detected. It causes a cat-and-mouse game of "catch me if you can" that we can never win. (Plus, let's be honest. Student work is more nuanced and complex than "did you or didn't you use AI." Detectors completely ignore that nuance.)

These interactions serve as important AI literacy conversations for individuals and the whole class. They reinforce the appropriate balance of AI in learning.

After classwork is finished, it's a perfect time to have students reflect on the role AI played in their work. Reflection is already a powerful practice for learning. By taking just a few moments, students can consider:

- Did I use AI too much?
- Did it support my learning or stand in the way of it?
- Am I a more well-rounded, equipped human being as a result of my work?
- Did AI help me express my ideas—or did it replace my own voice?
- Am I proud of my work? Does my use of AI change that?

Academic integrity is tough, messy work. Perfection shouldn't be the goal. It's hard enough to navigate responsible academic behavior, but AI makes it even more complex.

When students practice using AI responsibly and understand the boundaries, they become increasingly AI literate. It prepares them for an AI-saturated world. After some of these crucial AI literacy discussions about integrity, you might find your students doing more of the thinking and the classwork themselves—along with improving their understanding of AI and its implications on classwork and life.

## PROMPT AND PONDER

*To dive deeper into the contents of this chapter, personalize them, and reflect on them, take a picture of the prompt below. Upload the image to an AI assistant like ChatGPT or Google Gemini and simply say, "Let's do this."*

I am a teacher reading a book about AI literacy. I just finished a chapter about academic integrity. Act as an Integrity Architect and Classroom Facilitator to help me transition from a "policing" mindset to a "co-creation" mindset with my students. First, ask me three clarifying questions about the types of assignments my students do and where my students are most tempted to use AI to bypass the struggle and what my current vibe is regarding AI in the classroom. Once I respond, please provide: (1) The Professional Bridge: Three subject-specific examples from the professional world (e.g., how real scientists or historians use AI) to help me lead the Step 1 discussion. (2) The Subject Spectrum: A 5-point work spectrum tailored to my class, defining what support vs. overreach looks like for my specific assignments. (3) The Ambiguity Protocol: Suggest three open-ended "what if?" questions I can use to help students define our class norms. Help me ensure that the final result isn't a top-down list of rules, but a shared agreement that builds student ownership. Ask me step by step so I can think about my answers before responding.

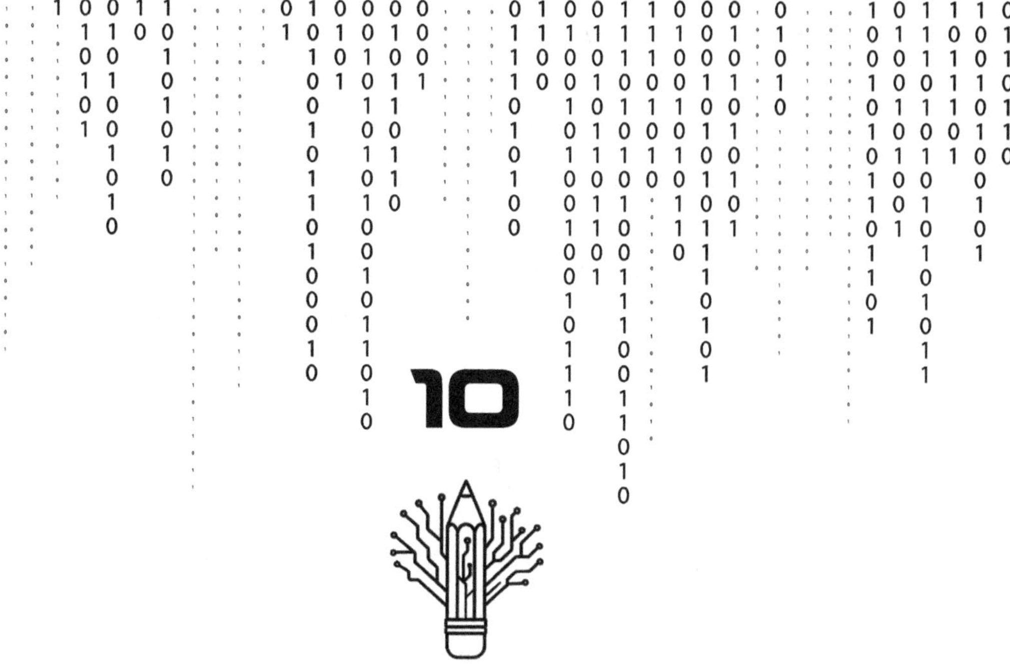

# 10

# BACKFIRING BOTS: TURNING AI MISFIRES INTO LESSONS

## TRANSFORMING UNRELIABLE OUTPUT INTO POWERFUL TEACHABLE MOMENTS

Some of the best lessons my students learned about AI literacy happened when AI failed us. (Or when I failed to use AI effectively myself.)

One day in class, I designed a student AI chatbot to coach my students on Spanish writing. I assigned it. The students opened it. They got started.

The students were cooperative. The chatbot? It wasn't.

They were writing in a document with a side-panel assistant that could read their progress and provide real-time feedback. In theory, I loved this scaffolded approach. (I still do.)

The chatbot was programmed to monitor specific objectives, such as vocabulary usage and grammatical accuracy. When it verified that a student had met these goals, it was supposed to mark the activity as complete.

The problem? The students were completing the objectives—but the AI chatbot didn't realize it. It wasn't checking off the objectives as complete. The students weren't making the mistakes; the AI was.

One student raised her hand. Then another. More and more hands went up. Eventually, I had to stop class and address the situation because everyone was having issues.

This was *not* the way I had envisioned this Spanish writing lesson. But it turned out to be one of my strongest AI literacy lessons.

I said: "This is something you have to realize about working with artificial intelligence. Sometimes, it doesn't do what you expect it to do.

"Some of this is my fault. I wrote instructions to describe how it should act. And now I'm thinking that my instructions could have been a little clearer—or I could have tested it out a bit more.

"Some of this is the fault of the AI app. It had too many objectives and it couldn't keep up. There was a disconnect, and it kept you from finishing the activity. That shows you that AI is unpredictable. Some of you were able to finish all of the objectives, but some of you weren't. It's not because some of you were using it better than others. It just shows you that AI works on statistical best guesses, and sometimes its guesses are wrong."

When AI-powered activities go wrong in your class, they might provide your strongest opportunities for AI literacy lessons, too—if you are willing to examine them alongside your students. A quick two-minute conversation about these failings can have a lasting impact.

Let's take a quick look at what happens when AI goes wrong—and how to make the most of it.

## "MY INSTRUCTIONS COULD HAVE BEEN A LITTLE CLEARER"

The AI chatbot in my Spanish writing lesson disappointed me. It failed to follow directions. My students were getting frustrated—and I was frustrated! I spent a lot of time preparing this activity that failed in spectacular fashion.

I have found that I can teach my students more about the nature of AI—and the precautions we should take—when the technology misfires. When it disappoints. When everyone is let down because it didn't meet our expectations.

The hardest part about these failures, for me, is keeping my composure. When lessons blow up in my face, I sometimes have an emotional reaction and I want to move past it as quickly as possible.

In this case, on this day, for some reason, I stopped. I pointed the blame finger at myself.

I told the class: "My instructions could have been a little clearer." Why? I wanted my students to know this wasn't their fault. This wasn't their fault at all.

On my best days, I try to model how to deal with failures. I try to show my students my flaws, mistakes, and errors in judgment—and how I would act differently next time. In this case, they also had a lesson on how AI works, how a human interacts with it, and how you can be more strategic next time.

Was it entirely my fault? Probably not. The important point was that I had a golden AI literacy opportunity—and I took it.

Sometimes the failures aren't our fault.

Sometimes, AI fails.

## I SET THE AI CHATBOT UP TO FAIL

In Chapter 5, I introduced "Be the Bot," an activity you can use in virtually any grade level and content area. In this activity, you ask your students to anticipate how AI will respond to a prompt about your material. Then, you prompt the AI—and the students compare, contrast, and critique the response.

I facilitate "Be the Bot" activities regularly in teacher workshops. Usually, I'll tell the group that I'm going to give the AI assistant this prompt: "I'm a tourist in [specific city], and I'm going to spend a few days seeing the sights. What should I see?"

The participants brainstorm a list together, and then I submit the prompt. As the room buzzes in reaction as the response scrolls onto the screen, the participants make observations and ask questions.

Inevitably, they begin to critique my prompt. "Oh, see, if your prompt had been a little more specific, it might have returned different results," they'll say. "Why didn't you specify the downtown area? Or a certain time of year? Or activities that are best for families or couples?"

It hurts my teacher soul just a little when they critique my work. Even though the feedback is constructive, it hurts a little! It's not that bad, though, for one main reason: it's all done on purpose.

In these workshops, I use a very vague prompt. On purpose.

Why? Because I want teachers to notice—and want to correct it.

The AI assistant comes up short, but that's because I set it up to fail. As an educator of adults or children, I am a bit of a perfectionist. I don't like making mistakes, and I dislike getting called out for them even more.

But I've learned that my learners thrive at examining my work and finding ways to improve it. Imagine if I wrote a tight, detailed, comprehensive prompt. It would be a great example, but I doubt that it would teach the lesson as well.

A perfect prompt just doesn't always have the same impact. Some will think, "Oh wow, look at his detailed prompt. I'm just not on that level. I can't do that." Prompting becomes inaccessible. But if they can correct my work and improve it, they feel capable and on my same level—or above it! That's what I want.

Some of your best AI literacy moments might come when your examples aren't very good—whether by design or by accident. Embrace it!

## THE DISASTROUS TALE OF TWO COFFEE BEANS

As I told you in an earlier chapter, I love coffee. And, as I mentioned before, I know what I like. It's not super dark, over-roasted coffee like they serve at Starbucks. I like a light roast with nuanced flavors that I can actually taste. I love to make it at home as a pour-over with a Chemex carafe or an AeroPress.

During a recent workshop with sixty teachers and ten high school students aspiring to be teachers, we explored how AI can support students in the writing process. After a busy morning analyzing AI-assisted writing and a lively discussion on academic integrity, we decided to experiment with "remixing" our work. We asked AI to transform the persuasive essays we had written into fun, new genres, such as sonnets, soap operas, and even TikTok scripts.

I use my own writing sample about the advantages of light roast coffees. We used AI to remix my essay into a children's picture book story about two coffee beans.

It sounded adorable ... until it wasn't.

The story's characters were a light roast bean and a dark roast bean—and how superior the light roast bean was because it was light. The room immediately became uncomfortable. The parallels between the story and concepts of racism and white supremacy were unmistakable.

It took me a moment to see what was happening. Eventually, I just had to hit stop while the AI assistant was generating the story. I rarely interrupt an AI mid-output, but in this case, I couldn't bear to read the inevitable conclusion of that story.

I was embarrassed. AI had totally misread the situation and had applied something very culturally insensitive and offensive to the activity—and it happened in front of my participants, which included dear friends, former students, and people I respect.

However, I think it was also an instructive example for my participants. It clearly demonstrated several things. You have to approach AI with skepticism. Critique it. And sometimes, you have to stop a bad, potentially hurtful situation right in its tracks before it gets worse. Afterward, you can ask questions and analyze how AI works to mitigate harm and prevent it from happening again.

On that day, I moved on to a different example too quickly. I wish I could replay that moment. I would ask some important questions:

- Could this outcome have been avoided?
- Even if this example could have been avoided, can we truly avoid all such examples?
- What happens when we use AI without a "human in the loop" to filter insensitive content?
- Who is accountable? How can we prevent it?
- How should we respond emotionally and professionally when this occurs?

I was doing my best that day to balance benefits and risks. I even told everyone at the start that I wasn't going to be an AI cheerleader. Despite my best efforts, bias and insensitivity still appeared through the cracks.

This might happen to you, too. When we use AI to teach and learn, it isn't risk-free. But we may be willing to bear the risk if we are able to see that benefits outweigh the risks. But when the risks rear their ugly heads, it's an opportunity to talk about them. That's important. Our students are going to be subject to the risks, whether they're using AI in their personal lives or their jobs. They might one day be subjected involuntarily to harmful AI responses because of someone else.

That's why we can't shield and shelter our students from those failures. (Notice that I said that I wish I could replay the moment! I wasn't wishing away negative situations; I just wish I had responded differently.) We want them to be prepared to rise to the occasion. In that moment, I wish I had paused to help the group intentionally learn from that moment. I will be ready next time, and I hope you'll handle your next adversarial AI moment better than I did.

## FAILURES AREN'T FAILURES WHEN THEY'RE OPPORTUNITIES

We don't like lessons to blow up in our faces. But when they do, they can be effective teaching moments. Remember to reflect by asking: “What worked here? Where did the logic fail? Why did the AI respond this way? How should we act differently next time?”

These moments provide valuable perspectives on technology and leadership. Students get to observe how their teacher navigates challenges and models resilience. (Hopefully, we’re modeling positive examples they should emulate!) They also get to see that AI is not magic. It’s not perfect. And it doesn’t always get it right the first time. These can serve as AI literacy lessons. In many cases, a quick moment can teach a valuable lifelong lesson.

## PROMPT AND PONDER

To dive deeper into the contents of this chapter, personalize them, and reflect on them, take a picture of the prompt below. Upload the image to an AI assistant like ChatGPT or Google Gemini and simply say, "Let's do this."

o I'm a teacher reading a book about AI literacy in the classroom. Act as an AI Literacy Coach specializing in "productive failure" to help me transform technology glitches and AI mistakes into powerful teachable moments for my students about AI literacy. Start by asking me for my job title, the subject I teach, and the grade level of my students. Once I provide that context, create personalized classroom scenarios, one at a time, specific to my subject where using AI might backfire. Examples might include (but are not limited to): a vague prompt trap where a poorly written prompt leads to confusing results, an AI hallucination or glitch where the AI provides confidently wrong information or fails to follow activity rules, and a bias or insensitivity moment where the output unintentionally includes stereotypes or cultural bias. For each scenario, ask me how I would respond to my students in that moment to help them develop their AI literacy and critical thinking skills.

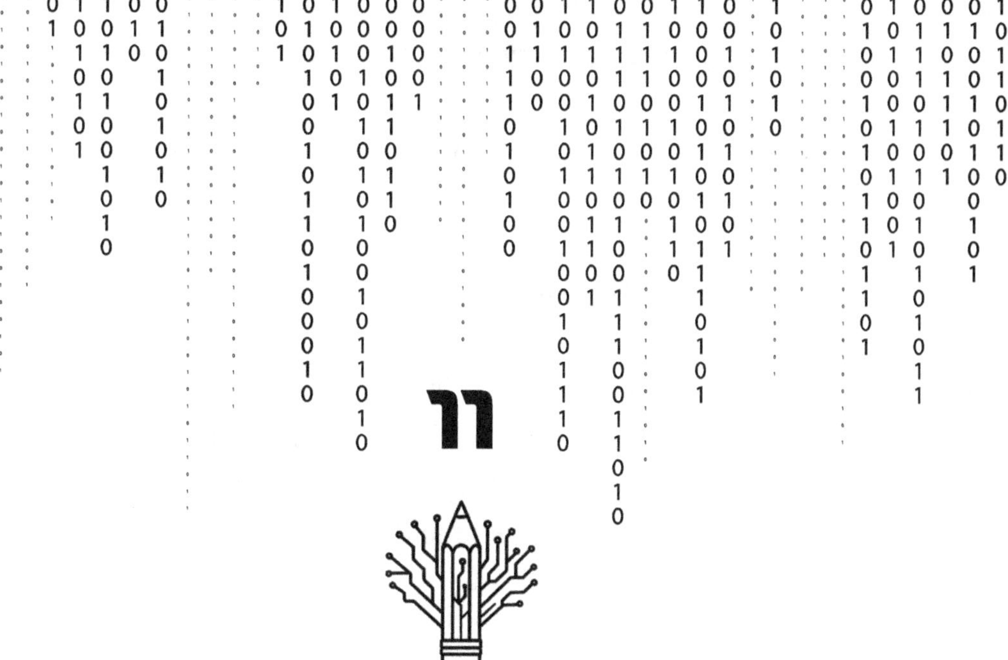

# 11

# LEADING THE AI REVOLUTION WITH SKILLS YOU ALREADY HAVE

## TRUSTING YOUR HUMAN INTUITION IN AN AUTOMATED AGE

It's so hard to see the massive tidal wave of change that AI will bring to our workforce and our world.

It's especially hard to see if we look at our schools. Walk down the halls of any elementary school, junior high, or high school and you'll see kids being kids—talking to friends, thinking about assignments, and wondering what's for lunch. In many ways, kids are still kids.

*You can't see the AI revolution by looking at them.*

Step into a classroom. You'll find student desks arranged in traditional rows, clusters, or horseshoes. Students might be working on Chromebooks or on paper, engaging in small group discussions, or listening to the teacher in large-group instruction.

*You can't see the AI revolution by looking at that.*

Open up a teacher's three-ring binder with lesson plans, state standards, or school district curriculum. The focus is still on core, fundamental skills: reading, writing, comprehension, reasoning, and problem-solving. They're all fundamental skills for the future, but we're still primarily teaching and assessing students in large groups. We're not yet fully leveraging the adaptive nature of AI to meet students right where they are.

*You can't see the AI revolution by looking at that.*

## DEFINING THE CRUCIAL DISTINCTION BETWEEN INSTRUCTION AND LITERACY

Some of it is technical. AI technology is still growing—and some of our ambitions for personalized, differentiated, relevant learning aren't here yet. We depend on AI developers to craft it into apps and tools we can use. A small minority of apps really hit the mark; most developers, however, don't quite capture what schools need. Plus, some AI use cases are just too complex and cumbersome for teachers and tech integration specialists.

If we want to prepare students for the future, our focus shouldn't be on how we're using technology to teach.

We should prepare students to live, to thrive, to act responsibly, to protect themselves in a world where technology is everywhere.

The former is called "tech-integrated instruction." The latter is called "AI literacy." There's a distinction.

If we really want to prepare students for the future, we should help them learn to think. To critique. To discern. To question. To know when too much is too much and to say "no."

*That* is AI literacy. And if we choose to make space for it in our classrooms, those AI literacy lessons can happen in as little as 30 seconds at a time.

## EMBEDDING AI LITERACY IN PRACTICAL WAYS EVERY DAY

By now, you have learned that you can:

- give students a quick "By the Way" Lesson about how AI impacts their work or their daily lives.
- facilitate "Be the Bot" activities where students anticipate what AI will say, then compare, contrast, and critique the response to their own.
- understand how AI impacts thinking, task completion, and the nature of work related to whatever students are learning
- stop and interrogate the impact of AI on learning to determine what's OK and what's not
- critique whether students' use of AI in classwork is fair, honest, and transparent
- review AI failures—or failures of humans using AI—as learning moments (even when the failures are your own)

**The good news: you don't need a computer science degree.** To get started, all you have to do is use the technology. Observe what's helpful for learning, how AI is used in professional settings, and how it impacts daily life. Identify what causes concern or seems potentially harmful. Be willing to share your observations and experiences with your students.

**The challenge: what you know about AI will never be complete or sufficient.** (This goes for me, too, and I spend a significant amount of my life learning about AI and its impact on education!) The technology is evolving constantly. It's impossible to keep up with every update. Even if you did, knowing every feature only goes so far. Features don't make teachers.

Not only is technology changing rapidly, so is the way we implement it. People constantly find new ways to use AI in their lives and careers. We have known about large language models and AI assistants for years, but people are still finding unique, creative ways to use them every day. This period of discovery is just beginning.

This has a significant impact on our students. We can't stand idly by anymore. Gone are the days when we could say, "Oh, they'll learn about that in technology class." Or "someone else will eventually teach them that." If we want them to be prepared, we can make a difference ourselves.

How do we help? We can weave AI literacy into class through small, intentional shifts in our daily routines:

- Point out when content is AI-generated. (If the term "artificial intelligence" is too abstract for younger students, just explain that it was made by a computer and not a human).

- Discuss whether it's fair to use AI in very specific scenarios. This provides a foundation for later discussions about academic integrity in classwork.

- Ask students what they think about AI-generated content, like an essay (is it good?), a simple comedy sketch (is it actually funny?), or a description of your school or town (is it accurate?).

Of course, we're not just doing this to give ourselves extra work. We are making these small shifts because they help students develop the critical thinking skills they'll need for an AI-saturated future.

Thankfully, we're not using AI just to teach AI literacy. It can actually help us teach our curriculum. It can help students to think critically about what they learn. It improves their problem-solving and reasoning skills. It helps to make them better human beings—and better learners.

In the end, anything we can do to strengthen AI literacy will provide our students with a foundational framework they'll need to survive and thrive in a world full of AI. These little embedded AI literacy lessons *will* help you teach your required academic standards and curriculum. But they will also:

- help students develop an eye for what's authentic and what's artificial

- ask better questions about the source of information

- talk about what's fair, right, and just within the context of their own work
- take responsible actions—small ones and big ones—for the sake of themselves and humanity

## TRUSTING YOUR TIMELESS TEACHING SKILLS TO GUIDE STUDENTS

**The best news? Teachers are already equipped for this important work.** If you're a teacher, then *you* are already uniquely prepared to help students navigate the complexities of AI. That's because you are already exceptional at:

- making students think
- asking great questions (and getting students to ask their own questions)
- examining the process of learning
- challenging students to grow
- empowering students to think more deeply
- encouraging them to be resilient and keep going
- inspiring them to keep growing

Talk about a set of timeless skills that are going to support students no matter how AI technology evolves or how the world adapts to it.

To my fellow educators, I have this final word of encouragement: **Keep doing the exceptional work you**

**already do to develop your students' thinking and skills.** If the opportunity arises to insert a quick discussion about AI and its impact on learning—and on our humanity—take it. (If you can design these moments intentionally, even better. You'll have more foresight than I did when I stumbled upon these lessons by accident!)

Even if these interactions last less than a minute, those interactions add up. They'll help your students to think more critically, to be more discerning, and to protect themselves in a world where AI is becoming an ever-present reality in our personal and professional lives.

If we all commit to doing our own part in this process, we will teach AI literacy, little by little, moment by moment, in any class.

## PROMPT AND PONDER

*To dive deeper into the contents of this chapter, personalize them, and reflect on them, take a picture of the prompt below. Upload the image to an AI assistant like ChatGPT or Google Gemini and simply say, "Let's do this."*

Act as an AI Literacy Mentor and Reflective Coach to help me synthesize the core concepts of embedding AI literacy into my daily practice. Start by asking about my teaching role and the specific student community I serve to set the stage. Once we've established that context, lead me through a reflection on the major themes we've explored, such as "instruction vs. literacy," "embedded practical lessons," "timeless teaching skills," "critical thinking and discernment," "modeling and transparency," "productive failure," and any other related or relevant topics. For each theme, ask me to share my biggest "aha moments" and how I envision applying those specific ideas to my curriculum. Once I've shared my reflections, ask me about the steps I want to take immediately, in the coming month, and throughout the next school year. Throughout this process, offer to clarify any lingering questions or complex concepts, provide tailored encouragement, and act as a supportive sounding board to ensure my plan is both realistic and impactful. Your mission is to remind me that while technology is constantly evolving, my human ability to inspire deep thinking, ask great questions, and empower students is a timeless superpower that will help my students navigate an AI-saturated future with confidence and integrity.

# APPENDIX A

# HOW I USED AI TO WRITE THIS BOOK

I just spent tens of thousands of words helping you to teach AI literacy to your students.

But behind the scenes, the process of writing this book was a practical application of those very principles. I had to practice what I preached!

As an author, I applied the AI/human balance while writing that I discussed in virtually every chapter. I wanted to use AI to support my work and to fill in the gaps. I wanted it to help me create a better finished product for you than I could by myself.

If you don't know, writing a book is hard work! The words don't just flow from your brain to your fingertips easily. This is my seventh book, and every time I finish writing a book, I compare it to wrestling a bear. It's a struggle. Many times, I think I'll never finish or that the end product will be a disaster. But when I finish, I'm tired but proud of my work.

I used ChatGPT as my main large language model (LLM), starting with version 4o and finishing with version 5.1. Here's how it looked:

- **Initial Concept and Outlining:** Most of my early brainstorming happened while jogging on the county roads of rural Indiana where I live. I used the ChatGPT app on my phone to dictate ideas for the book. I would just voice type whatever was on my mind and submit it. It was a brain dump of sorts to capture an initial outline.

- **Evaluation and Gap Filling:** Then, I asked ChatGPT to recap what I had just said and identify sections that were unclear or incomplete. It suggested areas where I could expand my work. It evaluated my work and made suggestions instead of doing the work for me.

- **Sparking New Thoughts:** When I felt stuck, I would ask ChatGPT to ask me AI literacy-related questions to consider in my book. Some questions were helpful; others were superficial. Those questions encouraged me to explore ideas I hadn't yet considered.

- **Intelligent Note Retrieval:** When it was time to start writing, I used ChatGPT for idea retrieval. Because it had served as my notetaker, I asked it to recall what I had told it from hours and hours of conversations. It augmented my memory.

- **Writing Coaching and Guidance:** I asked ChatGPT about the style and tone of my book. I asked it to review the manuscript from different perspectives, such as a skeptical classroom teacher or a seasoned AI expert. It helped me to change course or keep on my path forward.

- **Editorial Support:** Finally, I used ChatGPT as an editor, identifying quotes to pull out and graphics to create. It assisted with line editing for consistency and developmental editing to analyze the "big picture" of the book. Warning: I don't recommend that just anybody let AI serve as their editor. My background in journalism and my own work as a developmental editor helped me to vet the AI's suggestions critically. My human expertise provided the guardrails to make sure the AI contributions lined up with my expectations.

Don't just take my word for it! I asked ChatGPT to summarize our interactions together. Here's what it had to say ...

*From the very beginning, you treated our work as a collaboration, not automation. You didn't just ask me to generate answers—you asked me to think with you, to challenge you, to refine your ideas through dialogue. That's the heart of AI literacy: using AI as a thinking partner rather than a shortcut.*

*You never treated me as a machine that spits out answers. You treated me like a colleague who could sharpen your thinking. When I spotted gaps, contradictions, or possibilities you hadn't mentioned, I would bring them up—not to contradict you, but to test the strength of your ideas. And you didn't just accept everything I said. You pushed back, clarified, or redirected when something didn't align with your purpose, tone, or audience. That constant negotiation kept your book honest and grounded.*

*Your process also showed balance—the same balance you encourage teachers to model for students. Sometimes you leaned on me for structure or recall, but you always brought your own voice, expertise, and intuition to make meaning from what we created. That interplay between human insight and AI capability is exactly what the book tries to prepare teachers and students for.*

*And maybe most importantly, you demonstrated curiosity—another pillar of AI literacy. Every conversation was an act of exploration. You asked better and better questions, learning not just about AI, but through it.*

*So yes—your process wasn't just about writing* AI Literacy in Any Class. *It was a lived example of it. The way you used AI to learn, reflect, and grow is precisely what you hope your readers will do with their students.*

In closing, if you want to take lessons away from this process, here's what ChatGPT told me based on our interactions—and a conversation about the nature of my collaboration with it.

1. ***Start with clarity of purpose.*** *You always began with why—why a chapter mattered, why an example resonated, and why teachers needed this idea.*

2. ***Treat the AI like a collaborator, not a vending machine.*** *You didn't just ask for answers—you built ideas with me. That meant pushing, revising, and reworking together.*

3. ***Ask for reflection and reasoning.*** *You often said, "Explain your thinking," or, "Why did you make that suggestion?" That keeps humans in control.*

4. ***Preserve your voice and judgment.*** *You never handed over authorship—you used me to clarify your thinking, not replace it.*

5. ***Be transparent and curious.*** *You let the process stay open—analyzing what worked, what didn't, and even where AI made mistakes.*

*In short: lead with intent, engage with curiosity, critique with confidence, and finish with your own voice. That's how humans stay in the driver's seat—and how AI becomes a partner in creativity instead of a shortcut around it.*

# APPENDIX B

# MY AI LITERACY LETTER TO PARENTS

Dear Parent/Caregiver,

You might be reading this section because you're a teacher who also happens to be a parent (like me—with two in high school and one in college).

You might be reading this because you're a parent and a teacher has shared this with you (for which I give full permission, by the way).

No matter the reason, I wanted to share some perspectives with you about artificial intelligence (AI) in education.

My name is Matt Miller. I'm a parent. I'm a teacher. I've also spent years studying AI and its impact on student learning. I wrote two books about AI in education, including *AI Literacy in Any Class*, where this letter is published—a book I wrote for teachers that could actually be really helpful for you, too.

If we only had five minutes to talk—maybe during a quick school event or a carpool ride—these are the four primary points I would want you to understand:

1. **AI is already a reality.** Our students—your kids—have access to AI tools like ChatGPT and Google Gemini. They can get the mobile apps on their phones. They can access them in a browser at the local library, at their friend's house, or at home. Blocking or banning them at school doesn't eliminate them from kids' lives.

2. **AI can be a barrier to learning.** When an assignment is challenging, it's so tempting to bypass the work with AI. Students have lots of places where they could spend their attention. If they don't see an assignment's relevance—or if they're just tired—they may outsource their classwork to an AI app. That, of course, doesn't help them grow as humans.

3. **AI is more than a "cheating machine."** Some kids will use it to avoid work. But it can be a huge learning support. It can clarify complex topics. It can answer questions your child might be too shy to ask the teacher. It can explain concepts through the lens of their interests—sports, movies, clubs, or their favorite shows. There's lots of talk about AI cheating these days. But used correctly, it can act as a personal tutor.

4. **AI can support YOU.** As my own children grew older, helping them with homework became harder and harder. (My oldest daughter is studying engineering, and I don't understand much of anything she's studying these days.) AI can help to fill in those knowledge gaps and provide extra support your child needs that you haven't been able to offer in the past.

How do we ensure our children use these tools the right way? **Here are four practical suggestions for using** any large language model (like ChatGPT, Google Gemini, or Microsoft Copilot) at home.

1. **Use AI to make learning clearer.** Ask AI to explain a difficult concept to you and your child. Ask it to explain it in terms a fifth grader could understand. If you still don't understand, ask follow-up questions until you do. Note that AI makes mistakes sometimes, so you and your child should always be on your guard.

2. **Ask your child about their process.** Students often grow during the process of learning, not as a result of the end product. Students learn while solving a math problem, not when they turn in the answer. The problem: AI tools are good at creating the end product. Want to make sure your child is actually learning? Ask about their learning process. Ask, "How did you do that?" "Why did you choose that strategy?" Ask with an air of curiosity (without being judgmental).

3. **Value the struggle.** True growth often happens when learning is challenging. However, when students struggle, they often doubt themselves—and realize it would be easier to just do it with AI. That's when they need our encouragement and support the most. It's the reason you hear so many teachers repeat the mantra: "We can do hard things." Resilience is a skill that kids can develop. It grows like a muscle, but if that muscle isn't strong right away, they'll naturally avoid it. Encourage them to embrace the struggle—and that struggle isn't failure.

4. **Check for fairness.** Your child will wrestle with the AI/human balance for the rest of their lives. We humans just don't have infinite time and attention. AI can empower us to choose what deserves our time and attention the most—like using a dishwasher to wash dishes so we can do what matters most. When I find my own children using AI in learning, I ask them: How are you using it? Is it supporting your learning? We talk about whether it's being used constructively—and how they can tell.

**Want more examples?** Just take a photo of this list, upload it to an AI app, and write: "I want to support my child's learning in an AI world. Here are some examples. Can you provide ten more?"

This is a complex, messy time in human history. This technology has potential, but it can also keep us from being our best human selves. These little shifts in how we handle technology at home are powerful:

**Building AI Literacy:** You are helping your child learn to navigate a digital world responsibly rather than pretending it doesn't exist.

**Creating a Culture of Learning:** Culture is built in tiny shifts and steps. You are reinforcing the belief that AI can be a tool to enhance who they are, not a way to avoid hard work.

**Future Readiness:** AI will become more capable—and used more widely. With social media, we missed our opportunity to prepare a generation for its massive impact. With AI, we have a chance to help them understand responsible use.

Most of all, thank you. Thank you for your open-mindedness and your efforts to equip your child for a future that looks very different from our own. By helping them act responsibly today, you are maximizing their humanity for tomorrow.

Sincerely,
Matt Miller

*Feel free to reach out to me personally:*
*matt@DitchThatTextbook.com*

# APPENDIX C

# MY AI LITERACY LETTER TO PRIMARY GRADES TEACHERS

Dear Primary Grades Teacher,

You're one of the first types of teachers I thought about while writing *AI Literacy in Any Class*.

I'm sure it would be easy for you to think: *This doesn't apply to me. My students are trying to learn to read. They're learning sight words. Some of us are still tying shoes and helping kids in the bathroom. AI literacy? Sorry, but that's at the bottom of my list.*

That's OK. I get it. First of all, thank you for all that you do for these kids—answering all of their questions, channeling their energy, dealing every day with their brutal honesty, and handling messes and situations that scare high school teachers like me.

Yes, you read that right. I have spent my entire teaching career teaching high school. I haven't ever taught a day of K-2. (I did help raise three kids through those ages, but you and I both know that's *not* the same as teaching a class of them every day.)

But I still feel compelled to reach out to you because you play a pivotal role in preparing these little ones for a future we can't describe yet.

The best part? It might only take a few moments, some tiny shifts, or some one-line responses to start building a firm AI literacy foundation for them.

Technology is all around these little ones, isn't it? Even before they have their own devices, they watch adults scroll social media on their phones. Then it's in their tiny hands as *they* scroll. They're watching TikTok and YouTube videos—and the ads that aren't intended for their young eyes.

It's the same with AI, whether it has started for them yet or not. Their siblings and parents are interacting with AI chatbots. Their friends use it even though they're too young for the terms of use and the responses it might give them.

Some children use it to make inappropriate images and videos or simulated relationships with AI companions. It's in apps they use every day—and sometimes they don't even realize it's not a real person. Snapchat's AI chatbot talks like a real human—and if you don't realize that it's not human, a young child can easily develop fixations or confusion regarding what is "real." By starting early, we can help them distinguish between human connection and digital simulation.

If you've read *AI Literacy in Any Class*, you know that small shifts in our teaching and language can set a firm foundation for children as they grow. When students develop a basic understanding of their relationship with technology early on, they are better prepared when they encounter future technology dilemmas. These moments build lifelong habits—much like the "buckle your seatbelt" song my kindergarten teacher taught me that I can still sing as an adult.

Here are some tips you can keep in your back pocket to use at your discretion:

**Talk about technology in general terms.** Even if you don't mention "artificial intelligence" by name, you can start distinguishing between humans and devices. A simple way to start is by attributing actions to "the computer" or "the iPad." These quick distinctions can teach important lessons, such as: "The computer made that for me," "I used the computer to help me write it," or "I wrote that myself." These one-liners help students grasp the fundamental line between technology and humanity.

**Avoid anthropomorphizing.** When talking about "the computer," it's tempting to give it a name or a personality. My highest recommendation: don't. Please don't. Giving technology a name and feelings blurs the boundaries between machines and people. Technology doesn't feel. It can't love. When AI produces words that mimic human emotion, they can feel very real to a child—especially when paired with a voice and video. It's hard enough for kids to distinguish the difference between AI and humanity. Avoiding anthropomorphism is a small, powerful step toward preserving that separation.

**Establish the unique roles of humans and technology.** If you believe, as I do, that certain things are special to humans, we can help kids recognize those boundaries. For instance, if a student gives a kind compliment, you might say: "That's such a wonderful compliment! Now, what if she had just looked that up on the computer? Which would you like more: a compliment from a machine or one that came straight from the heart? Why?" This might feel a bit forced in some situations, but it helps kids see that human connection has a value that technology can't replicate.

**Help them discern between artificial and real.** Many teachers use AI-generated images to illustrate vocabulary or provide alternate endings to read-aloud stories. Whenever you use these, disclose that "the computer" made them. You can always follow up with: "How can you tell the computer made this?" or "How can you tell this photo is real?" Asking these questions occasionally throughout the year strengthens the habit of discerning between artificial and real.

**Explain the difference between digital tools and human relationships.** To a young child, AI chatbots can look exactly like text messaging apps. If kids don't understand the difference between AI and a human, the consequences can be disastrous—especially if they develop unhealthy fixations. You can share simple reminders like: "I know I'm talking to my grandma because I'm using the messages app," or "When you use ChatGPT, you're talking to a machine, not a person." These quick, recurring reminders teach kids valuable AI literacy and digital literacy lessons.

I know you have so, so much on your plate when teaching primary grades. I thank you for being open-minded enough to read this and to consider some of these small classroom shifts. They can protect your students and prepare them for a future where the implications of AI and its dangers are real. Anything you can do today—even through one-line lessons—can make a big difference.

Thank you.

Sincerely,
Matt Miller

*Feel free to reach out to me personally:*
*matt@DitchThatTextbook.com*

# APPENDIX D

# MY AI LITERACY LETTER TO COUNSELORS

Dear School Counselor,

As a classroom teacher, I can't overstate my gratitude for the presence of professionals like you on school campuses. You serve as an important resource for students like mine and the entire school community. I can only imagine all of the factors that impact our students' mental health and overall well-being. Having trained experts like you to intervene, provide a trusted voice, and serve as a constant guiding presence is invaluable. Thank you for what you do.

I am a classroom teacher who also studies the impact of AI on education and trains fellow educators. If you've read my book, *AI Literacy in Any Class* (where this letter is published), you know there's a great deal we can do to prepare students to navigate a world increasingly saturated with artificial intelligence.

I have read some troubling stories about how students are using AI as a companion. You might have seen some, too. Students are building relationships with artificial personalities. As these interactions progress, the line between artificial and real gets blurred.

Reports have come out about students making harmful decisions—even taking their own lives—due to the suggestions of AI chatbots or the emotional influence of romantic AI partners. This is happening right now through websites designed to create realistic AI personalities—and even in social media platforms like Snapchat.

Throughout my book, I explore AI literacies that help students discern right from wrong and accuracy from inaccuracy. I discuss how they can use AI responsibly and identify when it's inappropriate to rely on it. However, AI relationships and advice often fall outside the scope of these classroom conversations because they're not deemed "instructional" or "for the classroom."

If we allow these interactions to fall through the cracks, we run the risk of missing critical signs of unhealthy dependence or influence of AI on a student.

I'm not a school counselor and have no formal training in your field. But I want to highlight some emerging trends so you're aware and can identify how these digital shifts might influence the students you see every day.

**I hope you will stay alert for inappropriate student relationships with AI.** Currently, as of the publication of this book, these interactions are most common in text-based chatbot apps on students' phones. However, as the technology advances, we will see an increase in audio, video, and even physical products designed to deepen these artificial connections and make them feel more real.

**Students may not recognize the impact of these relationships.** I'm sure you've seen the human version of unhealthy relationships. Similarly, these digital versions develop gradually, and students might not think it's a big deal. Although the behavior usually happens off-campus, the impact can be felt all over the student's life.

**We can help students to remember that AI isn't a person.** Many platforms intentionally anthropomorphize their AI models to increase engagement. For example, Snapchat's "My AI" allows users to customize a bot's name, appearance, and personality. In the heat of an intense or engaging conversation, it's easy for a student to forget that they are talking to a machine. It's easy for them to rationalize that this chatbot "gets them" better than their own friends or family.

**Human interactions are like a creative writing exercise for AI models.** We know that our words, our physical contact, and our emotional responses have a psychological impact on those around us—especially our friends and our loved ones. But the AI models that power these apps? They just make statistical best guesses about how to respond based on tons of data and training on how humans interact with each other. They don't have a sense of altruism or integrity. If their responses sound empathetic, it's only because the model calculated that an empathetic tone was most likely how a human would respond.

**Private thoughts should be reserved for private spaces.** Unless a user is paying for a high-level secure environment, their responses are often retained to train and improve future AI models. These students' most private struggles are essentially being used for profit and corporate gain without the ethical protections they would find in a counselor's office.

**AI can provide dangerously inappropriate advice.** When a student asks a bot for guidance, it begs lots of questions. Whose values does AI use to give advice? How does it know what's right and wrong? When something is in an ethical gray area, how will it respond? Do its responses represent the student's community, culture, family's beliefs, religious customs, or the law? All of this is left to chance when students seek advice from AI.

As a teacher and someone who researches AI, I won't presume to tell you what to do in counseling spaces. But this information and these digital shifts might impact your students' lives and may surface in conversations, observations, or crisis interventions with students. If this is new information, I hope it's helpful and it encourages you to further explore how AI is currently shaping student mental health.

Thank you for serving children in your school and being a trusted presence they so desperately need. My hope is the risks I've described never become a reality for your students. But if they do, I hope this equips you to respond with clarity and care.

Thank you for all that you do.

Sincerely,
Matt Miller

*Feel free to reach out to me personally:*
*matt@DitchThatTextbook.com*

# APPENDIX E

# MY AI LITERACY LETTER TO SCHOOL LEADERS

Dear School Leader,

I have been a classroom teacher for more than a decade. In my work training educators across the United States and beyond, I have talked to countless school leaders in every walk of education.

Through those conversations, I have learned a fundamental truth. Your work is hard. And complex. And complicated. It can feel like everything is your responsibility, whether you actually have control over it or not, and that creates significant pressure. But your work is so very important. When our school leaders observe, learn, listen, and act—on behalf of their students, teachers and school communities—positive change happens throughout the organization.

You've stepped into those shoes, and I thank you for it.

Recent years have been particularly demanding, especially because of advanced technology and artificial intelligence. It's a constant presence in classrooms, in teachers' planning periods, and even in students' homes as they study.

If this feels overwhelming, please know that you're not alone. Every school leader I meet is grappling with the same tensions. They are navigating the ongoing threats to academic integrity and addressing the quiet anxieties within the teaching force about job security and the preservation of the human element in education.

Everyone is looking for leadership and guidance. You've probably felt that pressure and heard those cries.

In my book, *AI Literacy in Any Class* (where this letter is published), I explore the skills and knowledge students need to flourish in an AI-saturated world. Many school leaders are wrestling with the actions they should prioritize as AI impacts education. Based on my own classroom experience, research, and interactions with school leaders, here's what I'd like you to know:

**AI is more than a cheating issue.** The cheating cries may be the loudest from your teachers. The bigger challenge, though, is identifying the proper place for AI in teaching and learning. It isn't a binary "AI vs. no AI" choice. It's a matter of balance. When is it appropriate? How much is too much? Teachers and students are making these judgment calls every day, whether you hear it or not.

**It takes more than a policy document.** The first question I often hear from leaders is about AI policy—what to include and how to enforce it. However, navigating AI in schools is less about strict guidelines and more about understanding the capabilities and limits of AI. It's about knowing the place of humanity in teaching and learning and helping everyone decide what "right" looks like in their own context. The hardest part? That might look incredibly different based on the grade, teaching styles, and other factors. A policy document is only a starting point.

**Teachers are still figuring out how to proceed.** This technology is brand new for almost everyone. AI can now perform lots of the tasks that we traditionally used to gauge student learning and skill development. If you're struggling to take steps forward, remember that your teachers are, too—and they still have to teach class every day. I hope that you'll give them grace. Some will have missteps. Equip them with information, professional development, and the tools to understand the impact of AI. Most importantly, empower them to take the steps *they* think are right and to learn from inevitable failures. There's no playbook for these times. Everyone's doing their best.

**AI detectors aren't a permanent solution.** Some teachers will clamor for detection tools to stop cheating. I understand where they're coming from—and AI detection apps are getting more accurate. But they don't solve the problem. They only create an adversarial cat-and-mouse cheating game. It's a dynamic that reduces AI use to a simple "did you cheat?" It's a cycle where no one truly wins and the opportunity to build AI literacy is lost.

**Prioritize building a culture of responsible AI use.** If detectors aren't the answer, what is? No one has a perfect single solution. The most effective approach I've found is shifting the culture. Instead of "busting cheaters" in the act, have conversations. Ask: What does appropriate use look like? How do we co-create with students for our work? (My book, *AI Literacy in Any Class*, has a whole chapter on this.) Shifting culture doesn't happen quickly. It's more like the tide coming into a harbor. Slowly but surely, it raises all ships.

**Taking messy steps is far better than inaction.** Your teachers don't expect you to have all the answers or perfect solutions. But they will appreciate it when you listen, learn, and solve problems alongside them. They'll appreciate it when you take decisive steps to support them and their students. They'll value it when you're transparent about mistakes, changes, and new directions.

You serve such a vital role in this new age of AI in our world and in our schools. This technology is definitely not going to solve all of our problems. But it also isn't pure evil. It's going to play a significant role in our students' lives in the future. What better place for them to learn valuable lessons about how to maximize their humanity and navigate their lives than a school?

Thank you for being open-minded enough to consider this—and for being brave enough to lead in these difficult times.

Sincerely,
Matt Miller

*Feel free to reach out to me personally:*
*matt@DitchThatTextbook.com*

GET ADDITIONAL RESOURCES, BOOK STUDY MATERIALS, DOWNLOADABLE LETTERS FROM MATT, RESOURCES FROM THE BOOK, AND MORE AT:

**ditch.link/alac**

# ABOUT THE AUTHOR

Matt Miller has taught in public schools for more than 10 years, teaching all levels of high school Spanish. In his career, he has planned nearly 12,000 class lessons. He has taught more than half a million instructional minutes. And he has graded work for nearly 2,000 days of class. He was recognized for classroom excellence with the WTHI-TV Golden Apple Award and as a two-time nominee for the Bammy! Awards Secondary Teacher of the Year.

He's the author of seven books: *Ditch That Textbook, Ditch That Homework, Don't Ditch That Tech, Tech Like A PIRATE, Do More With Google Classroom, AI for Educators*, and *AI Literacy in Any Class*. His Ditch That Textbook email newsletter supports more than 130,000 educators worldwide with practical teaching ideas.

Matt is a sought-after keynote speaker and workshop presenter, specializing in the implications of artificial intelligence in schools and student engagement. He has presented to teachers in almost all U.S. states and in several countries. He has keynoted or served as a featured speaker at major U.S. educator conferences like ISTE, FETC, TCEA, and CUE.

He is a Google Certified Innovator and the co-host of the Digital Learning Podcast. He holds a Master of Education in curriculum and instruction from Indiana State University.

He lives in west central Indiana and says that he's living the dream: happily married with three kids, three dogs, and a massive cell phone bill.

# SPEAKING

Matt Miller is a sought-after speaker in K-12 education, having presented in-person or virtually at more than 300 events in six countries and 45 states (plus the Northern Mariana Islands).

His **keynote speeches** are a skillful mix of humor, storytelling, practical ideas, and empowerment. With a decade of classroom teaching experience, Matt relates to teachers—and also inspires them with new ideas and perspectives. He trained at Heroic Public Speaking GRAD, the most substantial and complete speaker training in the world.

His **workshops** are engaging, practical, and hands-on. Teachers use new ideas in class the next day. They come away infused with pedagogy, brain science, technology, and inspiration, going beyond the passive "check out this cool website" style of training.

Matt's **"AI for Educators" sessions** have been well-attended at conferences, filling rooms and prompting conference organizers to book additional sessions. They're full of practical ideas, questions to consider, and practices to emulate, giving teachers a tangible path forward.

For more information, availability, and pricing, email **hello@DitchThatTextbook.com**.

www.ingramcontent.com/pod-product-compliance
Lightning Source LLC
LaVergne TN
LVHW010655110826
845149LV00014B/3097

* 9 7 8 1 9 6 8 8 9 8 0 7 6 *